Home Management 101

"It's difficult to stay organized in today's fast-paced society. Organizing your home and family is one of the most important things you can do to save time and alleviate stress. Debbie Williams shows how to get organized and do it with ease based on her experience as a wife, mother and an entrepreneur. Her 'bright ideas' tips are practical and easy to follow."
Lillian Vernon, Founder and Chief Executive Officer, Lillian Vernon Catalogs

"As the working mother of four children under 8 years of age, I can use all the help I can find in getting our lifestyle organized. Debbie's helpful hints were not only easy to incorporate in our busy lives but practical. Too many times, experts offer advice that doesn't fit with the reality of family, career and self—*Home Management 101* was very different. You can really work this information into your schedule and come out with more time at the end."
Maria Bailey, CEO and Founder, www.BlueSuitMom.com

"Think nobody understands your organization woes? Think again...Ms. Williams hits all the targets with *Home Management 101*. She holds our hands through the process of breaking down our daily tasks into tackle-able parcels. I highly recommend this book to any parent or homeowner who has needed eight arms or split personalities to try to get it all done and put away."
Mia Cronan, MainStreetMom.com

"Williams' book is filled with organizing tips that are not only practical, but are also easy for any busy family to implement into

their households. And after following her suggestions in the chapter on office management, I found work space in my writing area, I did not think even existed!"
Priscilla Y. Huff, author of 101 Best Home-Business Success Secrets and HerVenture.com.

"You won't be able to put down this book if you're looking for a common sense way to better manage your home and your family life. Say you have no time to read? Consider *Home Management 101* an investment of your time. This easy-to-read book provides the recipe for organizing, with a list of simple ingredients, basic instructions and enough options to help anyone no matter how organized or disorganized they are. Debbie even shares a secret we organizers see everyday: The myth that whoever has the most organizing products becomes the most organized person. Wrong! Prepare to money, time, and your sanity by putting the family team and responsibilities into perspective!"
Pat Moore, the Queen of Clutter, Professional Organizer, National Columnist and Speaker, www.queenofclutter.com

"Home Management 101 provides practical and proven tips for keeping yourself and your family organized. By breaking the organizing process into simple, easy-to-follow steps, Williams makes getting organized not only simple, but possible."
Lisa Kanarek, home office expert and founder of HomeOfficeLife.com

HOME
MANAGEMENT
— 101 —

Debbie Williams

CHAMPION PRESS, LTD.

CHAMPION PRESS, LTD.
VANCOUVER, WASHINGTON

Copyright © 2001 Debbie Williams
All rights reserved.
No part of this book shall be reproduced, stored, or transmitted by any means without written permission from the publisher.
Although every precaution has been taken in the preparation of this book, the publisher and author assume no responsibility for errors or omissions. Neither is any liability assumed for damages resulting from the use of the information contained herein. For more information contact: Champion Press, Ltd., 13023 NE Hwy 99, Building 7, Suite 207, Vancouver, WA 98686

Reasonable care has been taken in the preparation of the text to insure its clarity and accuracy. The book is sold with the understanding that the author and publisher are not engaged in rendering professional service.

The author and publisher specifically disclaim any liability, loss or risk, personal or otherwise, which is incurred as a consequence, directly or indirectly, of the use and application of any of the contents of this book.

ISBN 1-891400-21-5
LCCN 2001086215

Manufactured in Canada 10 9 8 7 6 5 4 3 2 1   7 6 5 4 3 2 1

Dedication...

To my husband Barry and our son, David -
Thank you for inspiring me to be the very best I can be

Acknowledgements

Many thanks go to all those who have helped me turn my passion for organizing into a successful business, teaching others how to organize their homes and balance their lives:

To my mom, Jimmie Kiar, for teaching me the most basic of all life skills: clean as you go; and to my dad, Paul Kiar, for listening to my all my dreams and supporting my wild projects, To my friends and colleagues who reminded me that I have the ability to change the lives of others through my writing: Donna Murphy for her constant encouragement and advice, Marnie Pehrson who motivated me to write the first draft of this book (I believe her exact words were "just do it!"), and Karen Hicks who worked her proofreading magic to make my manuscript ready for submission. Lanita Filer Jones for reminding me to stay on my path, and the wonderful group of webmasters who kept asking me for articles until I realized I had a bookful of practical tips for parents. To my colleagues within the organizing industry who so boldly went before me, paving the way for my own success with their pioneer spirit: Sharon Kristensen Demere, Barbara Hemphill, Lisa Kanarek, Pat S. Moore, Julie Morgenstern, Harriet Schechter, Sunny Schlenger and Susan Silver. Thanks so much for sharing your organizational tips and business expertise with a newbie. Many thanks to my wonderful editor, Brook Noel, for believing in this book project and making it such a fun journey-- I can't wait to write the next one! And lastly, to my mentor and friend, Harriet Schechter, who continues to be a guiding light in my career. Without her team spirit and willingness to take the reins, I would still be writing this book rather than sharing it with all of you.

Contents

Chapter One: Let's Get it Together
    The Four-Step Process / 3
    Creating an Action Plan / 12
    Seven Strategies for Success / 16

Chapter Two: Home Management 101
    You Are Part of a Team / 20
    Preserve Your Space / 24
    How to Manage Paper Clutter / 25
    Vertical Organizing / 29
    Maintenance 101 / 30

Chapter Three: Conquering Common Clutter
    Put Order in Your Closet / 34
    Conquering Kid Clutter /37
    Conquering Kitchen Clutter / 47
    The Organized Collector / 62

Chapter Four: The Organized Parent
    Power Wheels: 10 Steps to Organizing
      Your Mobile Life / 64
    Organization For the New Parent / 68
    Holiday Organizing Tips / 70
    Time Bandits / 77

Chapter Five: Office Management 101
    Multi-Tasking / 88
    Form versus Function / 91
    Organizing Your Work Space / 92
    Your Virtual Desktop / 98

Chapter Six: From Here to There: Effective Time Management
    What's Your Passion in Life? / 101
    Goal Planning Made Easy / 103
    Scheduling Time for Work, Self and Family / 106
    Setting Priorities / 108
    Time Management 101 / 109
    Designing an Effective System / 112

Chapter Seven: It's A Dirty Job, But…
    Bathroom Basics / 119
    Spring Cleaning for the Housework Impaired / 121

Appendix: More Help for the Organizationally
    Challenged / 124

Closing Thoughts / 133

Chapter One
Let's Get it Together

If you are reading this book, you may have found yourself among the ranks of the organizationally challenged. You just can't seem to get it together, running in all directions as you try to balance work, kids, family, friends and spouse, while still managing to squeeze in time for yourself.

You are not alone! Many busy professionals feel just as you do. Entrepreneurs, full-time working parents, and those who work from home, all feel that they are stretched beyond the limits of their physical and emotional endurance at one time or another.

What if I told you there was a better way? What if I said that I could show you a system that would ease stress while allowing more time for those things you truly enjoy—such as family? What if I told you the system was inexpensive, simple and easy-to-implement? Well that's what I'm offering throughout this book.

HOME MANAGEMENT 101

As an organizational coach, my life's mission is to help busy parents manage their time more effectively, reduce the clutter in their home and offices, and live a more balanced life. This book is a collection of organizing tips and tools to help you in your quest to get it together. You too can learn the skills that it takes to be organized and teach your teammates how to help you run a smooth household. This book will show you how.

Many years ago, when I taught in a kindergarten classroom, I learned a valuable lesson: I was responsible for setting the tone or attitude of the children under my care. Believe me, it's hard to keep your cool when Kevin is dashing for the nearest exit, Jennifer just threw up on your shoes and Jason is huddled under the table crying for his mommy (not to mention the remaining 30 five-year-olds wandering around the classroom.) Did I mention this was only the first day?

None of the educational books, classes and lectures I had studied in college prepared me for the lesson I learned that day. I desperately wanted to hide under that table alongside Jason, but then my teacher-training kicked in and I was able to pull a few rabbits out of my educator's magic hat. I could lower myself to the standards of a five-year-old and raise my voice to regain control or I could quickly change the tone of the entire room with a single controlled movement.

Calmly and quietly, I turned off the lights. That's all it took. Immediately, every child in that room stopped in their tracks, turned to look at me, and waited. I quietly helped the children find their seats and resumed my lesson.

This is an extreme example and perhaps your household isn't as chaotic, yet you often feel the entire weight of home management upon your weary shoulders. If you don't share these feelings with your spouse and children, they certainly won't know how to help you. By communicating to them what needs to be done, who can help, and how often, the members of your team can lighten your load. You can maintain control of your home in much the same way that I conquered the chaos in my classroom, given the right set of organizing tools.

Theoretically, you should create a list of chores or procedures for your home or office and delegate as many of these tasks as possible, and serve as a supervisor to make sure things get done. But that would be in a perfect world, and things don't always go that smoothly, do they?

This book is about real-life, practical, easy-to-implement strategies for those of you trying to figure out how to balance it all. After 15+ years of studying, researching and regrouping, I've developed a system and helped parents throughout the country implement it successfully in their own homes. This book shares all the information you will need to create a successful, easy-to-maintain system for your family. By learning the basic skills of an organized parent, you can react in a calm professional manner so that you control your household, rather than allowing it to control you.

The Four-Step Process

My life's mission is to help others find the balance between an organized career and home. However, most of us don't want to invest much time or money to accomplish this goal.

You may find it encouraging that a few basic tricks will take you a long way. One of my most time-honored organizing tactics is

HOME MANAGEMENT 101

looking at all organizational tasks with a Four-Step Process, which I will walk you through. And no, this won't cost you an arm and a leg with organizing bins and fancy containers. Developing a personal organizing system quite often involves more creativity than expense.

Before choosing a storage option, you will need to thoroughly sort the items in your household. There's not much point in storing items that you don't need. Use this as a guideline: if you haven't used it in a year, chances are you never will. Get rid of anything that you haven't used for the past year, except tax and business documents. (When in doubt about which legal and personal documents to keep, consult with your accountant or tax preparation specialist.)

> **Bright Idea # 1**
>
> *Miracle Iron.* This is the lazy man's iron and my father's miracle cure for avoiding wrinkled laundry. If you have not folded, ironed or put away the last load (or was it two?) of laundry in your home, don't rewash and re-dry the already clean clothes—that's a huge time-waster. Save time and energy by tossing the entire load into the dryer with a damp towel on a warm setting for 10 to 15 minutes. (Tip: use a lint-free dishtowel to avoid pilling of your favorite shirts and slacks.)

My friend Sandy is a good example of the well-intentioned organizer who lurks in all of us. Ready to get herself organized, she raced to the discount store to take full advantage of the Rubbermaid™ sale. Who wouldn't be perfectly organized with a car full of totes and bins in every imaginable size? But six months later,

Sandy asked me to help organize her bedroom closet. She simply couldn't figure out what to do with all those wonderful products (which, by the way, are still stacked quite neatly, but unused, in the bottom of her crowded closet). The moral of the story is "sort before you splurge". Sorting will reduce your storage needs while saving valuable time and money.

The key to effective, lasting organization is based on four steps: plan, sort, organize and maintain. This process is as easy as it sounds, and it's fairly easy to remember, too. I tried to create a clever acronym like those used by my colleagues in the organizing industry, but I kept coming up with words like PSOM (pronounced POSSUM) and OPMS (which sounds like a curse or prayer, depending on your point of reference).

These Four Steps are a simple process, and once you learn the basic skills of project organizing, you'll be utterly amazed at how well it works.

Step One: Plan your course of action. If you skip this step, your home organizing project is doomed from the very start.

Don't try to organize your entire home or more than one room at once. Organizing is like any other DIY (do-it-yourself) project, in that you will have numerous interruptions, so include them in your plan. Determine which problem area is your absolute worst, designating that as your starting point or launch pad. Close your eyes and envision how you wish it looked every day. That's the goal you're working toward. Now block off short time periods; 10-15 minutes works fine if that's all you have available. Those little minutes add up to an hour, then two, and before long you've organized an entire room and made tremendous headway.

HOME MANAGEMENT 101

I've included an Action Plan in this chapter to help you with this step. Creating a strategy to complete your organizational goals is a guiding light in this mission.

Step Two: Begin by sorting the items in your cluttered little corner of the world. Tackle items one piece at a time, working around the room in a methodical fashion. You can go in a clockwise, counterclockwise or zigzag pattern–whatever is most natural to you. Sort first, and then worry about storage. Be sure to have plenty of large empty boxes labeled: TRASH, KEEP, SELL and UNDECIDED. Trash bags will work as a substitute for the boxes, but they don't stay upright and you may get discouraged early in your sorting project. Remember not to get too attached to anything you touch during this step. Later, during your break you can take the time to travel down memory lane and flip through Junior's baby book. Right now it's time for action!

This is one of my favorite steps in organizing because it's a no-brainer. Anyone can sort socks, shoes, shirts, papers, catalogs and so forth, putting like things together and tossing them into the appropriate boxes. Get the kids to help or invite a friend to join you. Listen to upbeat music to keep you moving and on track. Don't leave your sorting area to put things away, because inevitably you'll get sidetracked down the hall or in the laundry room, never returning to where you began. We all know the story of a doomed closet-organizing job: we pull out our clothes, dump them on the bed and begin sorting. Then we see something that just doesn't belong there, perhaps a roll of quarters on the closet floor or marking pen, and off we go to the kitchen to put it where it should go. Resist the temptation to stray. Stay on course!

> ### Bright Idea # 2
> **Save money and space by making your items do double duty.** Invest in a cardpunch for your business cards then file them on your Rolodex™ rather than buying a separate box or organizer. Create additional workspace in your kitchen, bedroom or home office by purchasing a rolling cart with a flat top. Use a bedroom closet to create a niche for hobby work; close the doors to hide work in progress when not in use. Folding screens are decorative and easily disguise a work area. A folding card table or banquet table can be stored under the bed when not in use, which is convenient if your hobby room doubles as a guest bedroom.

Before you can take the next step, you must do something with all those objects you've sorted. Let's start with the easiest first then work our way up to the more difficult (another effective time management tip). Take the Trash Box outside to your garbage can, dumpster or curb for pickup. Remove it from the room so that you don't have to deal with it taking up valuable space. That was easy, wasn't it?

Now it's time to move on to the Sell Box. Carry it to your car or van to drop off tomorrow at the resale shop. (Or delegate this job today to a spouse or teenager who keeps getting underfoot.)

Let's take another look at that Undecided Box. When you've gotten this far in the process, it's much easier to be brutal, tossing things you would normally treasure. If anything is left in the box, move it to the hallway for now–you can tackle it after your upcom-

HOME MANAGEMENT 101

ing break. See—this won't be too stressful. We're only on step two and you're getting a break!

That leaves the Keep Box, which is the only box of stuff you will be organizing today. Is it bigger than a breadbox but smaller than your car? Good, it's finally time to put to use all those shoeboxes, check register boxes, egg cartons, and wicker baskets you've saved throughout the years.

Step Three: It's time to get organized! Use items from your kitchen and office to contain the clutter you've sorted, keeping in mind that the most-used items should be easily assessable.

If you've done your homework properly, moving from Step 1 to Step 2, and didn't skip ahead to this step (Step 3), your organizing job isn't nearly as difficult as you thought it would be. This is where you assign a home for your treasured items to live, and to return to after they've been used.

Create zones or centers, much like in a classroom, to keep track of your household items. Store tools in the basement or garage, arts and crafts supplies in the hobby room or kitchen, and extra paper towels in the kitchen pantry rather than under your bed. Close your eyes, and picture yourself or your family using these items. A good example is Play-Doh™. Most parents store Play-Doh™ in the toy chest or closet shelf in their child's bedroom, but it's a forbidden toy and is only to be used when Mom or Dad says so. (I wonder why Johnny is so confused when he is scolded for playing with Play-Doh™ in his room, smearing it into the carpet and on the walls?) As the manager of this home, where would YOU like to see Play-Doh™ used? At the kitchen table, where

LET'S GET IT TOGETHER

crumbs can easily be swept with a broom and kept out of the carpet? Or perhaps outside on the patio?

By thinking about where items are actually used, rather than stuffing them in leftover storage space, you're assigning a home and establishing a good future habit. Now each time you and Johnny work with clay, both of you will know where to return the Play-Doh™ to its home on the upper shelf of the laundry room.

Oddly enough, we think about child-proofing cleaners and medicines, but not items such as pens, clay, paints and stickers. Of course, it only takes one unplanned room-painting party to remind you that permanent markers are indeed permanent, and should be stored up high and remain off limits, to be used only with adult supervision.

Use this visualization exercise with the remaining items in your stack that present a problem or dilemma if you are unsure of where they should be

> **Bright Idea # 3**
>
> Install over-the-door organizers such as laundry bags, bookracks, ironing boards and utility racks to keep your floors uncluttered and to further utilize unused space. Most stores now have organizing aisles with a large array of products from which to choose. Multi-tiered racks over your linen closet door create a quick medicine cabinet, instant pantry in the kitchen or audio/video library in a hall closet. (Great for apartment dwellers who have no wall space for a dedicated entertainment center.) Mesh laundry bags clip over your bathroom door, kids' theme bags hang on the doorknob and a netted basketball hoop attaches with suction cups to your child's closet door– Whoosh! He shoots, he scores!

HOME MANAGEMENT 101

stored. It's okay to think outside the box, and store arts & crafts in the kitchen or laundry room, not in the bedroom. Often storing medicines in the kitchen cabinet under lock and key makes much more sense for the parent of young children than putting them in the traditional bathroom medicine cabinet.

Use common sense organizing techniques to keep your home safe and stress-free. And don't be afraid to reorganize or move items around as the needs of your family change. Obviously, as Junior grows older, he can be trusted to refrain from marking on the walls or using the toilet bowl cleaner as finger paint.

Thinking in the zone helps with the long-term plan of getting your household in order, making room in specific areas of your home for baking, crafting, bill-paying and playing. Since these are action words, we may as well call your task centers ACTION ZONES.

The bill-paying action zone will probably be in your kitchen rather than upstairs or at the back of the house in the office. "Use it or lose it" applies to organizing as well as brain cells. So set up your newly organized house using common sense, as well as the new skills you have learned. Believe me, you'll thank yourself at the end of a long day.

Step Four: Keep up the hard work by maintaining your organizational system. This is perhaps the most challenging step in organizing. It's fairly easy to get organized, but how on earth do you stay that way? Remember all those creative ideas you came up with in the organizing step of your project: file boxes, binders, storage boxes? Those created a home for your papers and knick-knacks and that's where you will continue to place incoming items on a regular basis. Don't let this organizing step overwhelm you–it's simply a matter of cleaning as you go, and making an effort to put things back where they belong.

Some efficiency experts feel that "there is a place for everything, and everything in its place." But that would be in a perfect world. My home certainly isn't perfect, and I imagine yours isn't either! Instead of giving up before we even get started, let's walk through a typical day and its possibilities.

Upon waking, you use the last tube of toothpaste, so you make a note on the Toiletry Inventory Sheet hanging inside your linen closet door. While you're fixing breakfast, you realize you're almost out of milk and eggs, so you jot those items down on your Grocery List, which is posted on the side of your fridge. Everyone is able to sit down to a nutritious breakfast because clothes were clean, pressed and laid out the night before. No one misses the train or school bus because they made lunches the night before and stuffed them into their backpacks, adding completed homework to the pack and hanging it on the coat rack. Videos were returned to the video store on the way to work because they were tossed in the Out Box after they were viewed last night.

This may seem like a fairy tale or dream world, but many parts of this scenario can be played out in your own home if you use the organizing steps outlined in this book. Do I still have your interest? Good! Let's map out an action plan so you can turn this dream into a reality in your own home.

Creating an Action Plan

Before you can create your action plan, you need to evaluate the biggest organizational challenges in your home, then visualize how you would like to see those areas of your life changed in the not-too-distant future. For instance, if you face a pile of papers on your kitchen countertop each morning during breakfast, and it starts your day off on the wrong foot, then perhaps this is a good place to start your home organizing project (not in the attic that has remained untouched since you moved in). List five of your organizational nightmares and focus only on these areas for now.

THE TOP FIVE ORGANIZATIONAL NIGHTMARES IN MY HOME ARE:

_____
_____
_____
_____
_____
_____
_____
_____
_____
_____

Now that you've faced the clutter monsters under the bed, it's time to see things as you want them to be. Close your eyes and visualize clean surfaces free from clutter, with a home for papers, artwork, backpacks, keys and dirty towels. What are the dreams you have for your new organized home? List the top five below.

MY TOP FIVE ORGANIZATIONAL DREAMS ARE:

_____
_____
_____
_____
_____
_____
_____
_____
_____
_____

Your Personal Action Plan for Organized Success

Now that you've confronted your organizational nightmares and dared to envision an organized home of your own, it's time to create an action plan for success. This will be a four-step process where you will first identify the rooms needing an overhaul, then prioritize your step-by-step organizing projects, set goals or a timeline for completing each, and lastly document your success. Not only does your Action Plan have a grid to provide you with the big picture, but it enables you to monitor your progress and see how far you have come in your quest to live a more organized life.

HOME MANAGEMENT 101

Implementing The Four Step Process

Put a check beside all the rooms below that exist in your home. Focusing only on the items you have checked, choose the place you would like to begin and put the number "1" beside it. Find your second biggest organizing challenge and place a "2" beside it. Continue the prioritizing process until you have assigned a number to each room you have selected.

Set a realistic date to organize each room (numbered item), and mark that date on your planning sheet. Mark each room as it is completed and include that date in your notes. This will serve as a realistic guideline for future projects, and will also remind you that you can do this—and indeed you have!

Closets	Goal Date	Date Completed
___ Hall Closet	_____	_____
___ Linen Closet #1	_____	_____
___ Linen Closet #2	_____	_____
___ Bedroom Closet # 1	_____	_____
___ Bedroom Closet # 2	_____	_____
___ Bedroom Closet # 3	_____	_____
___ Bedroom Closet # 4	_____	_____
___ Hall Closet # 1	_____	_____
___ Hall Closet # 2	_____	_____
___ Other Closet	_____	_____

Bedrooms
___ Master Bedroom   _____   _____
___ Bedroom # 2   _____   _____

LET'S GET IT TOGETHER

___ Bedroom # 3   _____   _____
___ Bedroom # 4   _____   _____
___ Bedroom # 5   _____   _____

Bathrooms
___ Master Bathroom   _____   _____
___ Bathroom # 2   _____   _____
___ Bathroom # 3   _____   _____
___ Bathroom # 4   _____   _____
___ Bathroom # 5   _____   _____

Other
___ Garage   _____   _____
___ Attic   _____   _____
___ Basement   _____   _____
___ Living Room   _____   _____
___ Dining Room   _____   _____
___ Kitchen   _____   _____
___ Pantry   _____   _____
___ Breakfast Nook   _____   _____
___ Den   _____   _____
___ Office   _____   _____
___ Family Room   _____   _____
___ Porch / Sunroom   _____   _____
___ Bonus Room   _____   _____

HOME MANAGEMENT 101

Seven Strategies for Success

I have found seven strategies that are necessary for basic home management. They are easy to implement and will work wonders throughout your journey. Try to add one of these strategies to your management system each week or month.

- ❖ *Enlist Help* - Delegate jobs to other family members. You don't have to do it all yourself.

- ❖ *Double Duty* - Do two or more things at once: fold clothes while talking on the phone; file bills or papers while watching TV, etc. Many of you already practice this skill on an unconscious level.

- ❖ *Beat the Clock* - Set a timer for five or 10 minutes and have everyone clean up. Competition among siblings or against one's best time is a great incentive.

- ❖ *Block and Tackle* - Use 5-10 minute time blocks to tackle big jobs (cleaning closets, attic, basement and kids' rooms). The job will eventually get done and you will achieve a sense of accomplishment each time you work on it.

- ❖ *Ready the Troops* - Iron or assemble clothing for an entire week at a time. Make lunches the night before. Line up backpacks by the front door.

- ❖ *Clear the Decks* - Leave your home as clean as possible. Make beds and wash dishes before you leave for the day. This keeps you from being too overwhelmed upon your return.
- ❖ *Divide and Conquer* - Make a to-do-list at the end of each day, prioritizing with Must Do Today, Must Do This Week, Would Like to Do Today, etc. This keeps your tasks in perspective.

Sometimes we forget that the family unit is just that: a unit working together for a common goal. In this case, your troops can help you establish a workable organizing system. Try to be only as organized as you need to be and establish a routine that you know your family will use regularly. If you remember that being organized is an ongoing process, not an end result, together you can manage your household and the time that you spend as a family. Take action today by implementing one of these seven strategies in your own household.

Chapter Two

Home Management 101

When planning your home organizing strategy, remember to include a variety of tools and techniques to ensure success for you and your family. Not only do you need to de-clutter and find a home for your family's treasures but you have to be able to find them when you need them.

To ensure my clients create a customized organizing system, I've developed a simple system for organizing any project, from car to home office. There are four basic storage choices: Hang it Up, Put it in a Drawer, Store in on the Floor or Shelve It.

Hanging items on racks, hooks, doorknobs or in bins keeps them off the floor, creating more space for larger items and eliminating visual clutter. Putting kitchen utensils, office supplies and cosmetics in a drawer organizes them by size, shape and function—again eliminating visual clutter and keeping like items together. Storing shoes on a rack, archived bills in a box and seasonal cookware in stacking crates makes good use of floor space in a pantry, closet or work zone. And storing books, videos and household plants on shelves consolidates collections and utilizes vertical space where there was once chaos.

Using any or all of these tools in different combinations will help you develop an individualized working system that you will really use. Customize it to your own personality, preferences and lifestyle. If you don't like to dust, display your collectibles in a china cabinet behind glass. If you are concerned about bathroom germs, gather your makeup sponges and brushes and stash them in drawers. And if you need a clear workspace before paying monthly bills, store office supplies in a zippered pouch rather than utilizing coffee mugs for storage containers. Anything short of your own personal system will simply not work—you've "been there, done that" already.

File cabinets for your kids provide a safe place for papers that take over the house: school work, pictures, cards, awards and certificates, art projects and report cards. Use metal file cabinets or milk crates to hang bright-colored files, then label and fill. Don't just organize what they have accumulated, but rather work together to create a system of filing that they will use on a regular basis. Each time papers find their way home from school they can be placed in a folder, filed or returned to school when completed.

The Four Storage Choices

1. Hang it Up
2. Put it in a Drawer
3. Store in on the Floor
4. Shelve It

HOME MANAGEMENT 101

YOU ARE PART OF A TEAM

There is a motivational poster that reads: "The Word TEAM Does Not Have the Letter I in It". I first saw this in my son's preschool, but have since seen it in numerous bookstores and corporate conference rooms. Being part of a team means working together to accomplish a shared goal, not "hot-dogging". It works in the office, it works in sports and it can work for you and your family at home. Enlist help with routine chores and errands, and don't expect the same perfection from family members that you expect from yourself.

Enlist your 10-year-old son to shred papers in your overflowing trashcan. Teach your 12-year-old daughter the basics of filing by delegating this weekly routine task to her. Encourage teamwork in the home. No single person made the mess, so pitch in and help one another on a regular basis. Divide and conquer!

Being part of a team is much more than just sharing a name or hanging out together. It's using combined talents and energy from a group of individuals for the benefit of all. So how can you translate that into household chores that get

> **Bright Idea # 4**
>
> To further minimize storage needs, don't save magazines with dog-eared pages containing recipes, articles or tips. Instead, clip the articles then discard the remainder of the magazine. Store in magnetic photo albums or a notebook with dividers, or drop into a pocketed manila folder.
> This is yet another example of using the skill of effective sorting to save money on organizers.

done by the home team? Since you have already been appointed Team Manager it is your job to create an environment conducive to optimum performance and to coordinate the work being done. It's NOT your job to do every job involved in the project.

When's the last time you attended an amateur baseball game involving players over four-feet tall? Think back to those leisure years B.K. (before kids) when sports were fun. Someone was appointed (or self-appointed) to choose team players, assign positions and coordinate the baseball game. Usually this was the biggest or oldest kid on the block, who had experience and a gift for getting other people to do things for him. The Manager chose people to play on his team who could fill a need and were good at it. The kid with a strong throwing arm was first choice for pitcher, while others were chosen for catching, running or other athletic abilities. Then there were those of us who were willing to be part of the team, but were Second String material, always in the Outfield. Get the picture? Not everyone is great at pitching, but perhaps they're a great batter. And some people are better at distributing the bats or keeping score than catching a pop-fly in the outfield. But they're all a vital part of the team and can fill in where needed.

Call a family meeting, from the oldest to the youngest, to announce your game plan: Mom and Dad need to accomplish X amount of goals and need all the help they can get. Use visual aids, pointers or whatever it takes to get the attention of your spouse and kids. Hold all calls and keep it brief—no need to overwhelm them on the first try. Present a list of chores and ask for input on how often they need to be done. (Quite often this is a

HOME MANAGEMENT 101

learning experience for the Home Manager once she learns that her troops don't expect him to keep a shipshape house after all).

Once the chore list and frequency has been established, it's time to divide and conquer. Start with volunteers, going around the room to ensure each family member gets to choose at least one job they don't mind doing. Dad enjoys mowing the lawn to spend some time with nature. Sister would rather vacuum on a weekend than wash dishes after mealtime so she can talk with friends on the phone, and Junior likes water play better than dusting. Keep going around the meeting room until all the good stuff is gone then start delegating. Consider lifestyle, personality and schedules, and don't be afraid to be creative.

Now that your to do's have been delegated, the rest is up to them, right? Wrong! Your job as Manager has just begun, and you will need to routinely poke, prod and praise your kids and spouse into doing what you want them to do. Remind them that work comes before play; chores before video games and television. And tell them to keep in mind that if you have to pick up their slack (not to mention their dirty socks) you won't have time to drop them off at the mall or video arcade. If Dad forgets to pick up dry cleaning during the week, that cuts into his yard work time, which makes him late for the weekend hockey game with the guys.

Now the most obvious way to coordinate and manage chores is to nag, nag, nag. But we both know that just doesn't work (for long, anyway). This is not personal, but business, so let's use charts and graphs to keep things from getting heated. Using the information given to you by the team during your planning session (a.k.a. family meeting), create a list of things to be done. If your family is small, works well with little supervision, or you don't mind

HOME MANAGEMENT 101

micromanaging, then a simple running list posted in a central location (kitchen or laundry room) will do. List who is doing what and when, and leave it at that. It's up to the team to check the chart at the beginning of each week to remind them to do their chores, and it's up to you to make sure they're done. Verbal reminders and follow-up are fine.

But if your family is like mine, and not related to the Brady Bunch, then it's time to whip out the big guns and get down to serious household management. Purchase a blank chart from a teacher supply store, write down the names of each member of your family on one side, with the other side listing the chores needing to be done. Checkmarks or stickers will be placed in the gridsquare upon completion of the task. For older children and spouses, assign this job to them on the honor system. For smaller children who think this is a sticker game and will gladly fill up Daddy's Chart for him, retain this job yourself.

At the week's end make a note of empty spaces on the chart, and move on to the next step in your chore plan. Gentle reminders, loss of privileges and doubling-up on chores are effective ways to make sure renegade workers return to work duty.

The system is simple, effective and easily modified as your family grows and needs change. I highly recommend explaining your

> **Bright Idea # 5**
>
> Stacking cupboard racks expand your cabinet space, literally doubling the amount of items placed inside. Best used for dishes, pot lids, plastic wrap and spices, these can be moved from cabinet to pantry and back as your organizing needs change over the years.

system up front so there are no surprise attacks. Share with your family what needs to be done, what is expected of them and the consequences of not completing the work. It may be as simple as stating that if dinner isn't cooked, we just don't eat. Or if Dad doesn't mow the lawn, we'll get a citation from the neighborhood association, which Dad will have to pay for. Perhaps the consequences are more immediate and not as drastic, such as taking away gaming privileges from Junior if he doesn't take out the trash on pickup day.

Whatever you decide, try to stick with it for three weeks, and be consistent. Don't change the rules midstream until your family has a chance to decide for themselves whether or not this system works for the entire household. Be sure to follow-up on a regular basis with weekly meetings, monthly evaluations and quarterly sessions. Keep things simple and remember to encourage feedback from your team—after all, their job is to help you do your job better, so don't hesitate to change your game plan now and then for the good of the team. Use this type of teamwork to announce, recruit and manage your team players, cheering from the sidelines and giving pep-talks to promote team spirit.

Preserve Your Space

Once you've created a home and working system for items, share the information. Knowledge is power, as they say, and your family can't help you maintain your new system if they don't know what it is! Tell them where to put the mail, how they can find Spot's shot records and where you keep the hole punch. You'll be able to stay on task while they're grabbing the items they need. Or if you're not around when they need the information, they can easily retrieve it without putting out an APB (all points bulletin) for the item in question. Keep it simple, and stick with it.

How to Manage Paper Clutter

Paper overload is one of the biggest frustrations busy parents face. The promise of our becoming a paperless society seems to be only a myth. In reality, the cost of paper has considerably diminished over the past few years, making books, magazines, newsletters and direct mailings more affordable to publishers than ever. The advent of email and other electronic documents hasn't reduced our paper load, merely changed it, as we print out digital documents "just in case" or to read later when we have some down time.

However there are effective ways to cut the paper load in your life with little effort. I like to call it Preventive Maintenance. This means eliminating junk mail and faxes, creating a workable filing system and then filing on a routine basis. The short amount of time you spend submitting requests to paper producers is well worth the energy saved in the long run.

Short of hauling cardboard boxes over to help you sort through the deluge, I can help you learn how to trim the paper trail in your life. In fact, a basic filing method can be set up in three easy steps: 1) sort it 2) file it and 3) follow up on it.

HOME MANAGEMENT 101

Just Say No!

You can reduce paper clutter in your home or office by never receiving junk mail, faxes or telephone calls from solicitors in the first place. Following is contact information for the appropriate mailing lists to remove your name from those who inundate you with paper clutter:

JUNK MAIL: Mail Preference Service, 1120 Avenue of the Americas, New York, NY 10036-6700. (Special Note: When placing phone orders with vendors, request that your name be kept confidential and not released to mailing lists.)
TELEMARKETERS: Telephone Preference Service, P.O. Box 9014, Farmingdale, NY 11735.
JUNK FAXES: National No-Call Registry, 404.847.8785. Register your fax numbers with Technology Solutions International. Unless you are addicted to catalogs, you will be amazed at the change this makes in your mail sorting process. (Tip: if you enjoy reading catalogs for gift ideas or cost comparison, don't give up this hobby completely. Just do your reading online, saving a few trees, subscription costs and adding less to the landfills at the same time. Do the same for newspapers, newsletters and magazines, too.)

Mail Call

Choose a spot in your home or office to process or sort your mail each day, making it a natural part of your routine. Set up your mail station where it will actually be used, not where you think it belongs. Sorting by category reduces your processing time by more than half, and can be the most important step in organizing. Common mail categories include: junk mail, magazines, circulars, bills and reminders. Now turn these into your own categories for processing: Throw Away, Pay, File, Follow-Up or whatever you choose to name them.

Purchase colored folders for your mail center. After mail is sorted by category, place it in the appropriately labeled folder for action: green for bills, red for follow-up, yellow for filing, etc. Those of you who are visual learners can see at a glance where papers need to be filed, and can easily retrieve "pending papers" that have yet to be acted upon. If this is overkill for your own incoming needs, stand near the circular file (a.k.a. trash can) and file everything that isn't a bill or doesn't contain a check!

Sort it Out

Establishing a mail system is part of the paper battle, but now it's time to win the war with those stacks on your desk or countertop. However, it's not

> **Bright Idea # 6**
>
> Create a simple filing system using a recipe box and index cards or a three-ringed notebook with pocketed dividers. For bills and other correspondence, buy a notebook with twelve pocketed dividers, one for each month of the year. Label each with birthdays, anniversaries and billing due dates, then fill with your cards, invoices and letters. The binder can be used as a portable desk for processing bills in any room of the house. Designate one or two days each month to do your paperwork and you will avoid paying late fees and interest charges on loans or credit card balances.

HOME MANAGEMENT 101

time to make folders and file them away just yet. Before you can file a single piece of paper, you need to sort through the stacks. Get rid of anything that you haven't used for the past year, except tax and business documents. This applies to business and personal notes, magazines, newsletters, business cards, articles, sales leads and your Rolodex. Wondering what to toss and what to keep? A good place to start is with Publication 552 from the IRS, which can be read online and printed for further reference: www.irs.gov. When in doubt, contact your accountant for a list of documents to keep and for how long.

Did you know that eighty percent of what you file is never looked at again? This puts things into perspective, doesn't it? There are two basic file types: archive files and current files. Archive files consist of legal and tax papers that you are not actively working on but need to keep for possible reference or audit. Current files include: receipts, warranties, instruction manuals, reference material, client information, etc. There could possibly be a third category in paper management, hot files, which are works in progress.

Since each of us has different organizing needs, I can't offer a "one size fits all" solution, but I can give you some guidelines to help you come up with a system of your own making. Home managers, telecommuters, home business owners, small business owners with employees and CEOs of Fortune 500 firms have different filing requirements. If you're really overwhelmed and don't know where to put things even after you've read this section, it may be time to call for reinforcements. Don't be afraid to ask for help from a professional organizer, who can help you create order from the chaos you once called your office. Many professionals specialize in paper management or document control, which gives you an inkling of the demand for this type of service. You're definitely not alone!

Organizational specialists vary, as do your individual needs, and you can choose from a simple consultation to get you started to a complete organizational job working side-by-side or something in between. A good place to look for a professional organizer is in your community's service directory, local yellow pages, online or by asking a friend or colleague. My business, OrganizedU.com, provides free client referrals by phone, email, or through our online Membership Directory.

Vertical Organizing

This is the most productive step of organizing paper clutter, and consequently the easiest. Hopefully you have resisted the temptation of office supply catalogs and sales flyers urging you to get organized and buy more, more, more! As with the other projects tackled earlier in

---

Bright Idea # 7

Take Stock
A magnetic clip on the outside of your refrigerator neatly holds useful organizational tools in place: a grocery list, coupon envelope, toiletries list, freezer inventory, etc. Posting your list reminds you to make a note of things you need when you run out while streamlining the shopping process at the same time. On shopping day, just grab your list, a fist full of coupons and go! Keep a current inventory of freezer items, especially if you do bulk cooking, on the side of the fridge. Use a pencil so you can erase items as they are used.

the book, you need to thoroughly plan before you sort and by now your plan should be well underway.

Remember that any horizontal space in your home is a stack waiting to spawn baby stacklets of its own. Avoid future paper jams by creating vertical spaces for your papers, rather than horizontal ones. Store folders and reading materials vertically in racks rather than flat in a box or basket. Shuffling through papers is a big time-waster, and many important items can be hidden from your view. Remember the old time management rule: never touch a piece of paper more than once? Although it is outdated and difficult to follow, it does remind us to store our paperwork where it can be seen and processed without shuffling, stacking or shredding.

Sturdy magazine holders, desk organizer racks and wall-mounted bins are all effective organizing tools for paper storage. They not only contain the clutter, but also create more desk or counter space in your work center. Cardboard magazine caddies and plastic desk organizers may be a bargain, but may cost you more in the long run when you have to replace them often as they break. Plan your purchases wisely.

Maintenance 101

After you reduce the incoming paper load, what on earth do you do with the rest of it? It's now time to create a working follow-up system for your home or office, one that you will really use on a daily basis. This is the last and most crucial step to organizing your papers and time. Let's explore ways to keep track of projects requiring future action, those you need to complete or clients you need to contact at a later date.

- *File Box.* Purchase index cards with printed dividers. You can use an alphabetical system, (a-z) or write your own category name on the tab. Jot down important dates and projects on each card, then file away, keeping your file box within easy reach.
- *Accordion File Folder.* By an Everyday File, a 3-sided folder labeled A-Z or 1-30. Place each document behind the corresponding numbered or lettered divider. Keep only the current month in the dividers, placing the distant dates in the back of the folder. At the beginning of each month, pull the papers for the current month's attention and file behind the appropriate tab. (Note: as with hanging file folders, the dilemma of filing in front of or behind the tab is solely up to you. Just be consistent to avoid misfiled documents.)
- *Computerized Planner.* Purchase software designed for use alone or with a companion notebook organizer. Some programs include an alarm or flagging feature, which automatically notifies you of upcoming projects and their due dates. Depending on your level of technical expertise, this can be a PDA (personal digital assistant), a desktop computer, laptop or voice-activated recorder.

Make an appointment with your follow up file each day, ideally at the same time and place. By routinely checking your notes for calls to be made, appointments to be kept and clients to be con-

HOME MANAGEMENT 101

tacted, you will avoid missed due dates and having hot leads slip through the proverbial cracks.

Now that you've established your paper management system, let's think about maintaining it. Just remember three easy rules: 1) keep everything in its place 2) file as you go and 3) be consistent. Mail order catalogs are full of wonderful organizing products such as bill-paying notebooks, greeting card files, budget managers and planning calendars. Discount and office supply stores sell a variety of magazine holders, file crates, vertical file racks, wicker baskets and stacking trays. But don't go running to your favorite retailer every time they have a "Get Organized" sale. Many of these products are impractical for your organizing purposes. Start with one or two simple organizing items that really interest you; if they work, you can add more.

Efficiency experts tell us that it takes 21 days to create a habit. Try to stick with your new paper management routine for at least three weeks to ensure it is the right system for you. If it doesn't work, then by all means, modify it! Be sure to share these changes with other members of your family so that they don't unwittingly sabotage your system. Remember to only be as organized as you need to be. Tackle those stacks of paper ten or fifteen minutes at a time, each day, until you can finally see your desktop. I think you'll be surprised at how much you get done in a short time. Once you've set up your working system, commit to maintaining it. You will reclaim lost time and energy to spend on the things that are really important to you and your family.

Chapter Three

Conquering Common Clutter

The wonderful thing about effectively organizing your home is that you are learning the styles, principles and techniques of organizing. Rules, regulations and absolutes haven't worked for you in the past, and that's why we're here right now, working on this project together.

The organizing techniques in this book provide you with the recipe for organizing, a list of ingredients and basic preparation instructions. It's up to you to mix it up a bit, adding your own creative flair here and there. You wouldn't add garlic to brownies, anymore than you would add automotive parts to your bedroom closet—it just wouldn't set right in the pit of your stomach.

There are numerous ways to organize the chaos in your home, whether the clutter is in your kitchen, closet or bath. Rather than using tunnel-vision-organizing, which restricts your clutter vision and keeps you from seeing the big picture, adjust your sights and allow for creative organizing. Each room of your home is separate, and presents distinctive challenges for the best of organizers, but the principles are the same—expandable shelf racks organize kitchen spices in the pantry just as easily as toiletries in the linen closet. Hanging Dad's baseball caps from a hat rack in the garage works just as well for hanging jewelry in your teenager's bedroom.

Don't be afraid to use what you have around the house to contain the clutter. Instead of tossing that stack of wicker baskets in the garage, salvage a few for storing Sister's makeup or Brother's Legos®. Use your imagination to practice whole-home organizing, rather than micro-organizing, to ensure your organizing system will run smoothly and spill over into all the other areas of your busy life.

PUT ORDER IN YOUR CLOSET

For closet-organizing projects, let's revisit the four general-storage choices: hang it up, put it in a drawer, store it on the floor or shelve it.

For starters, gather several boxes and label them as before: Keep, Trash, Sell/Give Away and Undecided. Begin sorting. Just like before, don't try to find a place for everything until your items are sorted. Group your items by category: shirts, pants, shorts, T-shirts, jeans and sweat suits.

Decide what will be folded, what will be placed on hangers and what will go into drawers. By planning wisely during your sorting process, you have eliminated the need for many storage items. Use what you have around the house, buying specific-sized containers for the remaining items needing to be organized.

Up Off the Floor

Use multilevel rods to hang items. Bins and shelf dividers keep folded items neatly stacked. They are inexpensive to buy and can usually be found in discount or home stores. The time you waste rummaging for purses and other stacked accessories makes the small investment for bins and dividers well worth the cost. This will not only free up valuable drawer space, but can actually eliminate the need for a chest-of-drawers altogether.

Just Hanging Around

Use plastic coat hangers for ties and belts, and shoe organizers for shoes and purses. Shoe bags can be found at dollar stores. The smaller ones are sold from mail order companies and home furnishing stores. Hooks for caps, bags, umbrellas and purses keep things in sight for quick retrieval. (If you can hook it, you can hang it.) These are great space savers, and also make for faster, hassle-free retrieval.

Use over-the-door organizers such as laundry bags, book-racks, ironing boards and coat racks. Utility racks are excellent for storing tapes, compact discs and cleaning supplies. Hanging organizers with clear plastic pouches organize and display at the same time. These have small pockets for jewelry or larger pockets for shoes, pantyhose and

> **Bright Idea # 8**
>
> **Closet Tip**
> Use corrugated wine boxes, a hanging jewelry organizer or plastic fishing box for small treasures.

HOME MANAGEMENT 101

handkerchiefs. They also make an out-of-sight replacement for your junk drawer.

Depending on the climate, you may want to box up out-of-season clothes. Label the boxes and the contents clearly so that you can change your wardrobe easily as the seasons demand.

A hanging storage closet system is a great portable alternative to built-in organizers. These hook over your closet rod and have multiple milk crates suspended below. If you live in an apartment or move frequently, this is a cost-effective solution to shelves and cubbies. For kid's closets, hang this unit on a lower rod, and then move to a higher rod as they grow.

Use basic principles of closet organizing for each closet in your home: linen, clothes, coat and crafts. I recommend that you break down closets separately on your master plan as these tend to be at least half-day jobs. All of us have the tendency to put all the "I don't want to deal with it" items in the closet—making it a bit more of a challenge when you finally choose to deal with, and organize, them.

Don't try to tackle organizing every closet in your house at once. Use time blocks of 10-15 minutes a day until one closet is

---

Bright Idea # 9

Closet Tip:
When organizing your closet, group your shirts together. Sort by color, casual or dressy styles, long-sleeved or short-sleeved. Do the same for skirts, dresses, slacks and jeans. If you maintain this system, you can tell at a glance what article of clothing you need before you go shopping. You may also find you already have four white dress shirts and don't really need another one!

organized, then start on another one. Set a realistic goal, perhaps one closet a month. Before you know it, you'll find yourself well on the way to becoming a bit more organized.

CONQUERING KID CLUTTER

Lack of storage space is the number one complaint I hear from parents, especially in their kids' rooms. But organizing a child's room is just like de-cluttering any other room in the house: you have the same four storage choices: hang it, put it in a drawer, store it on the floor or shelve it!

Hidden Helpers

Footlockers or old-fashioned steamer trunks are great for hiding extra bedding and out-of-season clothes, but be sure to make them safe for small children by installing locking safety hinges. Stored at the end of the bed, the flat trunk lid makes a nice bench, or shove it

---

Bright Idea # 10

Unless your child has a student desk with ample drawer space, you may need additional storage for school supplies such as pencils, pens, paper clips, rulers and scissors. Why not utilize the dead space behind the door by hanging a vinyl pouch organizer on the bedroom or closet door? Most of these organizers hang the full length of the door, just begging to be filled with all sorts of treasures. But if your little guy is short in stature and can't reach the entire length of the door, use a jewelry-organizing bag instead, which is more compact.

HOME MANAGEMENT 101

under a window toped with a comfy cushion for an instant window seat.

Store markers, crayons, drawing paper, coloring books, beads and other craft supplies in plastic tubs under your child's bed. Be sure to label the end of the box or tub so your little Picasso can easily find her supplies when creativity strikes. This is also a good spot for the treasure box, which holds items that are too bulky or haven't yet found their way into the scrapbook.

When your child has outgrown the crib and is ready for a bedside table, top a lidded garbage can with a table round for functional storage. You can also create additional storage by placing a large bed sheet over an inexpensive wooden round table from your neighborhood discount store. There's no need to hem the sheet, just tuck under the edges for a puddled effect.

Need a place to corral those videos and books? An over-the-door storage rack makes an instant audio/video center, doesn't cost a small fortune and conserves wall space. You can easily find these in home stores, mail order catalogs and some discount stores. If your children are small (or very strong), consider reinforcing the bottom with screws to prevent the unit from slipping each time the closet door is opened. My son is no Hercules, but when he was three, he constantly opened and closed his closet door, and I worried about the unit falling down on his little blond head. I used wood screws to anchor the unit, making it more stable and giving me peace of mind.

Canvas or vinyl shoe bags can also be hung on the closet door to corral all those Beanie Babies®, Barbies®, and action figures scattered across your child's bedroom floor. Dollar stores, discount stores and home stores sell various styles, but the child-sized ones are ideal for small spaces. (And you don't have to worry about them swinging back and forth each time the door is opened). Remember that out of sight is out of mind, and even the best-organized room is useless if Junior doesn't use your new system!

For the Clothes Horse

There is absolutely nothing worse than the sound of a high-pitched child's voice whining, "Mom! Where are my gym socks? I can't find my gym socks!" Unless you live in a perfect world that no one else knows about, the socks are lost in the laundry room hiding behind the washer, clinging to your nylon gown or are on the dryer waiting to be paired up with their mates. So after clean clothes make it to their proper home, make them easy to find at a glance. Divide by color, dress or casual, and either roll them up or fold them neatly in a drawer. To keep them together, purchase drawer dividers for socks, underwear and other items, or make your own dividers by recycling heavy cardboard shirt boxes leftover from Dad's Christmas present. Place gym socks in one, dress socks in another, underwear in one or two, and so forth. This is also a great way to contain leotards and pantyhose for your little ballerina.

    Install inexpensive closet organizers for hanging clothes, which can literally double your child's closet space. Purchase a kit from the local DIY (do-it-yourself) store for permanent installations, or a free-hanging unit for a portable solution. Portable crates hang together, three or four units long and hook over your closet rod.

These are good for those living in apartments, base housing, condos or anyone needing a quick solution for their kids' closets.

Double up the horizontal space in your child's closet by hanging a second clothes rod parallel to the existing one. Not only does this quickly provide additional hanging storage for clothes, but it organizes them by function: shirts, blouses and tees on top, pants on the bottom. When your children are small, they can really benefit from a low-hung clothes rod that can easily be reached by the tiniest of tots. It instills a sense of responsibility in your little organized one, encouraging her to put away clean clothes, while enabling her to pick out her own clothes each morning.

Provide each child in your family with a laundry basket in their bedroom, or hang a laundry bag from their door. This keeps the clutter off the closet and bedroom floor, and also solves the problem of an overstuffed hamper in the laundry room or family bath. As the children reach adolescence or their teens, a full bag can serve as a reminder for them to start a wash-load so that they don't run out of blue jeans or tee shirts. The issue is more about accountability at this point, than containing clutter, but if they are already in the habit of putting dirty clothes away as they are used, then the next step is an easier one for the entire family.

An under-the-bed-box is great for temporarily storing outgrown clothes until you can sell or give them away, creating additional closet space. I recommend that you do invest in a sturdy long-lasting plastic tub rather than one constructed from flimsy cardboard. When the box is full transfer the clothes to a cardboard container and drop it off at a resale shop or charity. (Tip: Take the time to make a written list or inventory of items you are dropping off which can be signed and attached to your receipt. You may forget all these details when tax time rolls around.)

Follow the Paper Trail

Teach your kids how to manage the papers in their lives by providing a home for them. Create a sturdy desk by placing a wide board or door over two short file cabinets. Doors can be found inexpensively at salvage yards, garage sales or by driving around your neighborhood on garbage day. Spruce up with a couple of coats of fresh paint, some decals or stencils, and you've recycled a plain old door into a desk that will last for many years. Let the kids roll up their sleeves and put their creativity to work with handprints, sponge painting or the like.

Contain Yourself

Remember all those plastic tubs with lids you bought on sale? You know the ones–they're stacked in your closet or the trunk of your car? This is the time to put them to good use. Blocks, doll clothes, small toy cars, modeling clay and all the other loose items floating around the house belong together. I strongly recommend using shelves with tubs of different sizes as opposed to toy boxes. Toys last longer when they're stored gently and not stacked, and the kids can find things easier. Small plastic shoeboxes are perfect for doll clothes and cars. Purchase totes a size larger than shoebox size with handles on the top for easy carrying to and from the play area. Larger tubs hold blocks, play food and dishes, and other pieces that seem to multiply in the night.

HOME MANAGEMENT 101

Flat under-the-bed boxes are wonderful for out-of-season toys. Most closets are not large enough for toys and clothes, so why not store unused toys as you would clothing: kites, beach gear and baseball gear are stashed during winter months; footballs, hockey sticks and ice skates are stored during the summer. Try to buy clear tubs for easy viewing or label with words or pictures for younger children. If they can't see what's inside, chances are they won't use the toys within the nicely organized containers. (Kind of defeats the purpose, don't you think?) Get creative, and let the kids help you label the boxes with photos or magazine clippings of the items. It's a good rainy-day project and promotes reading skills for the little ones.

What's Your Hang-up?

One of the key rules in organizing and decorating is to utilize vertical space. Often we place furniture around the room with nothing above it, forming a nice horizontal line. There is a ton of unclaimed storage and visually appealing space right above the furniture line!

Hat racks, expandable or pegged, make wonderful hooks for stuffed animals, dress up clothes, hats (I just had to state the obvious here!), jackets,

> **Bright Idea # 11**
>
> Utilize jumbo tubs for train sets, car tracks, doll accessories and sports gear. For children five and under, rotate the available toys every one to three months, storing others in a bin. This keeps children from becoming over-stimulated while offering a change of pace.

backpacks and book bags. Smaller items can be hung to organize them by function: sports gear (baseball hat, glove, cleats) or fashion (jewelry, belts, scarves, hats). I once saw an entire wall of a kid's room lined with pegged hat racks, creating a chair rail affect. The pegs were at eye level for the little ones, who hung stuffed animals, hats, block-filled tote bags and various lightweight kiddy treasures.

To further utilize vertical space, install shelves and paint them to match the wall. Hang toy hammocks for stuffed animals. Spray paint a long shower tension rod, wrap with Velcro strips and stick up stuffed animals. Old soda crates found at flea markets can be cleaned, painted and will house treasures of all kinds: collections of shells, rocks, key rings, kids' meal toys and so forth. Smaller versions can be purchased at craft and discount stores. Interior decorators encourage us to keep our collections, but to consolidate rather than scatter them for a more dramatic presentation.

Encourage your child's creativity by enlisting their help for novel storage solutions. Give children a budget, make a list of things to contain, and see what they come up with. Perhaps they'll surprise you and suggest taking a boxful to their favorite children's charity or have a garage sale to raise money for newer toys. Involving your kids in the planning, prioritizing, sorting and containing stages ensures better (not perfect) participation in the maintenance of clutter. And who knows? You may actually nurture a minimalist of your own in the process or a packrat with incredibly organized closets!

HOME MANAGEMENT 101

Up the Down Staircase

How many times have you heard the back door open and close during a warm summer day? In Texas where we live, the flies come in and the air-conditioned air rushes out. Not a good thing! Toys in the hands of an active child follow the same rule and inventory has to be taken at the day's end to make sure baseball mitts are not left outside and bubble mowers are not dripping on the carpet.

Assign house rules and stick to them: inside toys, outside toys, upstairs toys and downstairs toys. Often this is a safety factor, such as all toys that can be thrown are outdoor toys (balls, bats, and horse shoes). All paper or cloth items are indoor toys (books, dolls, etc.).

If you have a two-story home, upstairs toys should not be dragged downstairs but remain in the bedroom or playroom. Keep a few toys on a small shelf, in a wicker basket or toy bin downstairs in the family room. Set a rule that these must be cleaned up each night before bedtime. Downstairs push or riding toys must stay downstairs and off the steps.

Keeping it Clean

In the primary grades, classrooms are set up in learning centers such as the Art Center, Science Center, Language Arts Center, Reading Center, Homemaking Center, Creative Play, Dress Up Center, Kitchen Center, etc. Educational experts have found through the years that organizing toys and props make a child's environment more conducive to learning, creativity and free play. Why not use this organizational technique in your own children's rooms to contain the clutter and encourage independent play in your household? Here are some ideas to help use this successful system inside your own four walls.

ART: Create an art center with crayons, drawing paper, markers, easel and chalk, Magna Doodle™, Lite Brite™ and other artist supplies. If you don't have the floor space for an easel, consider painting a closet door or short wall with chalkboard paint, give your child some colored chalk and let his imagination run wild. Just be sure to explain to him that not all walls are used for drawing!

READING: Turn an unused corner of the room into a cozy reading nook. Place a child-sized bookcase or freestanding milk crates along the wall, filled with books to read alone and together. Provide your literary genius with a beanbag chair, rocker or oversized floor pillow to plop down on when he's ready to curl up for a good read.

NATURE: Consolidate nature and outside play toys together in crates, tubs and boxes for your little naturalist. Magnets, a compass, magnifying glass, telescope, binoculars, kaleidoscope, a butterfly net and other tools for exploratory play develop his natural curiosity. Keep them in a box with a handle or on a small table to promote creative play.

DRAMA: Promote dramatic play by purchasing puppets for your little actor or make your own from socks, lunch sacks, wooden spoons or Popsicle sticks. Transform an appliance box into a puppet theater or drape fabric over a low-hung tension rod in a doorway for family productions. Gather old clothes, hats, coats, shoes and bags from Mom and Dad's closets for dress up. Better still, raid Grandma's attic or Aunt Agnes' trunk for shawls, hats, gloves and beads for hours of creative fun!

I think by now you get the gist of the learning center example–keep it simple, easy to access and easy to put away.

One Toy or Rotation Toys
Classroom teachers generally have a strict rule to contain the clutter in their classrooms. They must or they would spend more time cleaning than teaching. With young children, you may try several systems before finding the one that works best for your little clutterbug, but don't give up.

My mother had a "one toy rule" in our house. I had to put each toy away before taking out another. This may seem strict in your own home and does not work with every child. I was an "only", so this was pretty easy for her to enforce. With my own son, however, I began with the three-toy rule: he could play with three toys, then put them away before dragging out others. It worked well with puzzles, books and other like items. Then as he grew, and had toys both in the playroom and his bedroom upstairs, I implemented the "container rule": once the container was full, he had to stop bringing toys downstairs from his room. If he wanted more toys, together we could take the container upstairs and find new toys to play with. If you start these guidelines young, they may continue this clean-as-you go rule throughout life.

Or perhaps you like the "rotation rule" instead. Put only a few toys out on the shelves or in a basket for younger kids, then replace each week or two with new ones. This doesn't mean you have to go out and buy new toys each week, but pull toys out from your archived stash. Not only does it contain the clutter, it also keeps your kids from being over-stimulated with too many toys. A variation to this rotation rule is the "company's coming" rule: take out special toys to be played with in groups or when company comes to visit and play. Board games, badminton, bowling pins and other group activities are extra special to your little one when only played with occasionally.

Be sure to provide ample shelving, simple containers and practical solutions for your own rules. I found when my son was an infant that board books fell right through the slatted bookcase in his room, so I found stacking bins in primary colors for the smaller books. We use the bookcase for large toys instead. Feel free to bend the rules over time and create new ones as your child grows and his taste changes.

CONQUERING KITCHEN CLUTTER

Did you know that 20 percent of the total items in your kitchen are used 80 percent of the time? Wow! If we only use 20 percent of the stuff in our junk drawers and pantry, then why on earth do we feel the need for more storage space? That's a good question and one that I'd like to address by giving you some tips to help you reclaim some of the cabinet space in your kitchen.

HOME MANAGEMENT 101

The first place to start is the pantry or food cupboard. It's time to pour a cup of coffee or glass of iced tea, grab some boxes and get down to business. For most of us this is a no-brainer: toss old food, donate unopened dry goods and cans to food kitchens, and then organize the rest. Others just can't seem to get past the fact that they are throwing away or wasting food, and hear their mother's voice reminding them of starving children in Africa. But unused food is a form a waste, so you have my permission to sort, toss or recycle the unused food in your own cupboard.

Sort diligently and unemotionally, tossing items into the DONATE box that you know you and your family will not eat—unpalatable brands of meat, soups or vegetables that were on sale but were even rejected by the dog. Then place opened containers on the kitchen counter or floor to deal with all at once: pasta, rice, beans, sugar, flour, cereal, etc. Trash the obvious empty containers, or those you know are way beyond their fresh date (last year's Rice Krispies™ used only for Christmas baking, bran cereal you bought for your Dad before his visit last spring, etc.) Your UNDECIDED box shouldn't be very full after this kitchen organization project—it's difficult to get emotional about a bag of beans!

Take the DONATE box to the car, grab the trash box and let's tackle that huge row of boxes and bags lined up on the countertop. Before you begin filling up that neat cupboard, why not take a

> **Bright Idea # 12**
>
> Over-the-door hangers or door-mounted holders easily display pantry items. Holders for seasoning envelopes, spice boxes and plastic wraps consolidate these elusive items once and for all.

moment to wipe down the shelves with a whisk broom or damp cloth. Who knows when you'll pass this way again! Now it's time to consolidate, downsize and reorganize the containers of food that will reside in your pantry.

Some of you will be able to purchase plastic containers that are perfect for pouring cereals, keeping bread fresh and serve as canisters for baking needs. Others can make do with coffee cans, ice cream tubs or twist-ties. Any budget is enough to organize, just be creative and make do with what you have. The key here is to take action, conserving space and preserving freshness at the same time. This will save you time and energy searching for the right item for Grandma's cookies, not to mention prevent you from buying another bag of brown sugar because you couldn't see what you had in the shelves of your cluttered pantry.

The Spice of Life

Speaking of spices, being organized does not mean that you have to alphabetize your spices or use only what can fit on a nice decorative rack from a gourmet shop. However, it does mean that you should purge your spice collection on a regular basis; once or twice a year should do. Spices and herbs lose their effectiveness and potency with age, and if stored improperly near a heat source (beside or over the stove, for example), they quickly get stale. Put bagged spices into clean recycled spice jars and label clearly. If you desperately need more space in your pantry or cupboard, consider purchasing or making a spice rack to allow for more food storage space. My favorite organizer for spices is an expanding rack that looks like stair steps–the unit has three tiers and expands horizontally to fit almost any width. Although I purchased mine from a kitchen specialty store, I've also seen these in the organizing section of local discount stores. As you place your spice jars in your cupboard, group by category such as spices & herbs, sweet & savory, and so forth.

The best system is the one that works and that you will keep using. Change it as your needs change, moving large bottles to the back and smaller jars to the front for easier viewing. Just try to keep things cleaned out on a regular basis and return them to their proper home after each use.

Paper or Plastic?

When tackling the dishes, glasses and cups in your kitchen cupboards, take a good long look at your current dining conditions. Mentally form a picture in your mind of the average meal with your family. Do you only use paper plates, plastic cups and paper towels at the kitchen table each day? Then perhaps it's time to move that ceramic place setting for eight to the china cabinet, or store in the attic until your next dinner party. A good example of re-evaluating your needs is my friend Eve.

B.K. (before kids) she set her dinner party table creatively with a medley of cloth napkins, candles and either china or nice stoneware. Dinner was served in the formal dining room on the glass-topped table. Now that she's the busy mother of two, she has replaced those breakables with paper plates, paper napkins and sippy cups. Neither style is right, wrong, innovative or lazy. What works at the moment, for the varying ages and stages, is what's right for you. The main thing to remember is not to take up valuable storage space with items you no longer use on a daily basis. If you do use the stoneware and serving pieces for family Sunday dinners, keep them off-site in the dining room sideboard or in a box stashed in your coat closet. Or if you have older children and only use paper goods for picnics and takeout, keep these items across your kitchen in a less accessible cabinet, such as over the stove or refrigerator.

Refrigerator Clutter

Anyone who spends any time at all in a kitchen quickly learns about refrigerator art: what it is, how it's displayed and who created it. If your refrigerator is anything like that of other parents, it's plastered with kid art, the family calendar, homework assignments, soccer schedules, doctor's appointment reminders, and...that's just the front!

My refrigerator is full, too, but I gave up rearranging those teeny magnets ages ago. No sooner would I get six of them to hold up one tiny school picture, than SLAM–there went the whole arrangement crashing to the floor. Below are some of my favorite tricks of the trade to start taming the fridge clutterbug in your home.

ART DU JOUR: Instead of turning the front of your refrigerator into an art gallery, why not limit artwork to one per artist, saving the remaining paintings for Grandma or the scrapbook. Rotate the pictures daily or weekly, store in a tag-board portfolio beside the refrigerator and then move them to a more permanent home (like a treasure box or scrapbook). Hint: place your budding artists in charge of this project, letting them choose one day a week to change the artwork. Create a "home" for un-displayed work to live after its served time in the magnetic gallery.

PHOTO MAT: Consider using magnetic-backed acrylic frames to display your favorite snapshots. These come in various sizes for your photos, from wallet to 8x10. Or consolidate your pictures into a collage mat. Purchase these ready-made from catalogs or make your own by backing them with heavy-duty magnet sheets purchased from your local craft or discount store.

CLIP ART: Purchase extra-strong magnetic clips to hold important papers. Think of this as a vertical clipboard where you can post grocery lists, soccer schedules, homework assignments, signed field trip releases and copies of your latest dietary requirements. Not only does this conserve precious space, but also if your magnet is strong enough, you can just flip to the page you need with little rearranging.

CHORE CHARTS: Eliminate the need for repeated note posting and use a pint-sized chore chart for your family. I found a small wipe-off board shaped like a pencil in the school supply section of a

> Bright Idea # 13
>
> Purchase a package of sheet protectors at your local office supply store and place them in a three-ring binder. Use this to store Picasso's art. It keeps the pictures safe and easily fits onto a book shelf for easy storage instead of creating a pile of papers to shuffle throughout the years.

discount store, complete with grids, stickers and erasable marker. This particular product is backed with strong magnets, but you can easily add your own to a poster or homemade chart. If your kids are small, you may want to hang this high to avoid creative rearrangements of the stickers.

ABCs AND 123s PLEASE: Let's take a quick poll to see how many sets of plastic alphabet magnets you purchased before your kids reached adolescence? I'll bet that if you pulled out the refrigerator from the wall or used a coat hanger, you could fish out enough ABCs to write the Gettysburg Address. Why not use an alphabet poster instead, with medium-strength magnets attached to the back? Take a quick road trip to your nearest school supply store, and you will find posters on any subject that your child is interested in: alphabet (upper and lower), numbers (1-10, 10-20), farm animals, manners, The Five Senses, etc. I think you get the picture. It's much easier to corral a poster than a menagerie of plastic parts. Once Junior is old enough to use those plastic letters for spelling words, he's outgrown the fridge easel anyway and can easily use a laptop magnetic board or one that is mounted on his wall.

With a bit of creativity and a lot of consolidation, you can regain control of your refrigerator for the purpose it was intended: to keep foods cool and provide nutritional snacks for your family. But what should one do with all of Picasso's work? I'm glad you asked.

HOME MANAGEMENT 101

Portfolio: Create a simple art portfolio for each child in your family by taping two pieces of poster board together on three sides. Leave the top open for dropping in artwork as it is produced.

Each time your child brings home treasured work, date the back in pencil (or save time with the use of a date stamp). Then drop it into the portfolio for safekeeping. Or date it, then replace the display-of-the-week with the new one and file the old one away.

The end of each quarter or semester marks the time to purge your child's portfolio. Begin by sorting by type: paintings, drawings, collage, mosaic, seasonal, writing samples, tests or awards. Next choose a sample from each category, perhaps several scattered throughout the school year. File the keepsakes, discarding the rest. If you can't bear to throw them away, recycle by donating to relatives. Mail in a cardboard tube or ship flat between two pieces of cardboard. Your little Picasso's original makes quick and inexpensive wrapping paper, too. Another alternative is to scan the artwork, email it to relatives and throw away the original. Convert that scanned graphic into note cards, stationery or greeting cards.

> **Bright Idea #14**
>
> Create labels for relatives and friends and put some 9 x 12 and 10 x 13 envelopes in your child's portfolio. This will make it easy to send pictures to relatives when the portfolio is full and you need to free up space.

If your child can't bear the thought of you tossing any of her artistic samples away, delegate this task to her. Move the storage into her bedroom with her other belongings, and let her be in charge of sorting, dating, stashing and purging. Favorites can be archived into a scrapbook. It is amazing how quickly they will decide to part with things once their closet fills up faster than they can organize it!

Treasure Chest: Purchase a stackable cardboard storage chest from your favorite organizing company, such as Lillian Vernon or The Container Store. These sturdy units have removable drawers to fill with archived treasures and then stack vertically to conserve space. Use it as a primary storage system or in conjunction with the portfolio system. A frugal and creative alternative is to cover an unused pizza box or small flat box with colorful contact paper, assigning one box per school year.

A Picture is Worth a Thousand Words (and a lot of space!): If storage is a concern, photograph your child's artwork and discard the original. Either take individual pictures or line the artwork up for a group shot. Keep a disposable camera nearby, or use a Polaroid™ to take them individually. Dedicate a special photo album or box for these treasures to be shared and enjoyed for years to come.

Kid Kitchen Clutter
What kitchen in a busy household would be complete without the Tupperware™ cabinet? From the time your little one can crawl until he's ready to go off to school, having a dedicated kid cabinet (or drawer) will keep the clutter at bay and your sanity in check.

HOME MANAGEMENT 101

Provide your children with a space all their own, a low cabinet stocked with pots & lids for music development, plastic tubs & lids for matching games (early math skills), tea sets and cups for tea parties (language development and socialization skills) and art supplies. Change the items in your kid cabinet as your child's interests change. Keep it interesting and you'll have a safe haven for your little one to explore during those long hours on kitchen duty.

Coupon Capers

I feel compelled to include a brief commentary on coupon-clipping. Are the savings worth the time and effort? And if you clip—how do you organize?

When I first set up housekeeping, I did indeed spend a dedicated amount of time clipping coupons from the Sunday paper inserts and the Wednesday flyers. I methodically sorted the stack of coupons by category and placed them into the coupon wallet given to me as a college graduation gift from my mother. Each time I sat down to add new coupons to the organizer, I pulled out the expired ones, then moved older ones closer to the front so they could easily be seen. However since my family is currently on a special low carbohydrate diet, consist-ing mainly of

> **Bright Idea # 15**
>
> Swap coupons with a friend or relative and have fun with this project. Many moms and dads find this a thrifty hobby, or creative outlet. Reward yourself for a job well done with the money you saved and buy yourself lunch or apply that amount toward the family vacation.

CONQUERING COMMON CLUTTER

> ### Bright Ideas #16 & #17
>
> ***Cookbook Consolidation:***
> Most of us only use a handful of recipes from each of our cookbooks. Go through and take out the pages that you use and place them into a master binder. Buy clear page covers at your local office supply store to protect the pages. Create another folder for recipes you'd like to try and discard the rest of the book.
>
> ***Mark It:*** Recall recipes by book marking the pages with Post-It flags or colored paper. The colorful tags sticking out the top of your cookbook will serve as a reminder that you really *do* have an answer to "what's for dinner, Mom?"

fresh meats, produce and dairy, I no longer find coupons to be of personal benefit for my family's needs–I just can't find the coupons I need to match my menu and grocery list. So at this time I do not clip coupons.

However, I do highly recommend it for those of you who use a lot of mixes, prepared foods or condiments. The savings can be substantial, especially if your local grocers have Double or Triple Coupon days. Practice makes perfect, and you will need to diligently clip and store your coupons to make this worth your while.

One woman I know let's her daughter clip the coupons and be "in charge" of them during grocery shopping expeditions. For every used coupon, the daughter receives half the savings. This encourages her daughter to look for items they use regularly, helps teach savings and allows both mother and daughter to put a little extra money in their pockets.

HOME MANAGEMENT 101

Keep your wallet, envelope or other organizer up-to-date and carry it with you when you shop so that you can find the best buy for your money. If you have a small family to feed, and prefer certain name brand items, consider pulling coupons from your supply as soon as you post an item to your grocery list. At first you may need to double-check to make sure you haven't forgotten any coupons for needed items, but eventually you will do this routinely. This eliminates the need for carrying a bulky coupon box or file with you in your grocery cart. If that seems like too much work for you, consider keeping it in your glove compartment and just taking it out to refill—that way you'll have it when you are at the store.

> **Bright Idea # 18**
>
> Look in RV (recreational vehicle) catalogs and websites for space-saving products such as those mentioned above.

Cookbook Storage

Cookbooks have become all the rage for collectors—whether it's a collection of regional cookbooks collected on your travels or a mix of old homemaking books you inherited from Aunt Agnes. Where on earth do you store these collections? (Note: A collection is defined as two or more of one thing, so yours probably qualifies.) Sometimes it's easier to store all your books on the living room bookcase, including your recipe collection. This does keep them from getting dusted with flour and doused with cooking grease, but doesn't help you in your quest to create those Kindergarten Learning Centers, does it? If you are in the baking center preparing for your annual bake off, wouldn't you rather have all your recipes in one spot, rather than trekking all over the house for them?

Depending on your organizational style, you can easily find a nearby home for your own cookbooks in the kitchen. Make use of unused cabinet space over the refrigerator or stove by storing your cookbooks horizontally, with the spine on the outside for easy reading. (Most of these cabinets are not tall enough for vertical book display.) Or purchase a large flat basket and stash your books upright on top of your refrigerator. It's a much prettier display than the usual hodgepodge of cereal boxes and the basket makes retrieval much nicer. I advise against using bookends since each time your teenage son slams the refrigerator door, Betty Crocker will go flying across the room! However, you can use metal or heavy plastic bookends to consolidate your cookbooks atop the kitchen counter or a wide window ledge.

> Bright Ideas
> # 19 - #22
>
> **Crafty Storage Solutions**
>
> Hang a knotted rope or dowel rod horizontally to dispense spools of ribbon.
>
> Use toilet paper rolls to organize stand-up items (paintbrushes, scissors and pencils) in shallow tubs or totes.
>
> For glues and paints, make a three-sided box with 45 degree slanted sides and notched back for upright bottle storage. This makes a sturdy, portable work station.
>
> Tackle boxes are great for storing needlework. They are portable and small trays are perfect for needles, thread and buttons. Film canisters store small buttons and empty thermometer cases with lids are ideal for long needles.

HOME MANAGEMENT 101

Bright Ideas # 23 - #25

An Unjunk Drawer?

It's time to address the junk drawer. In the past, some experts have said "thou shalt not have a junk drawer in thine kitchen." Perhaps you've been diligent but unsuccessful in this task, and your junk has migrated from the kitchen drawer to the desk drawer or just sits in a heap atop the clothes dryer. There's simply no need to do away with your family junk drawer entirely. Just use any type of plastic basket or cutlery organizer for your junk drawer to categorize your junk, and clean it out routinely.

Use small baskets or a divided desk tray to group like items together, such as paper clips, rubber bands, twist ties, matches, pens, scissors, hammer, nails, screws, etc. During your monthly cleaning, remove the items that don't belong, such as broken hardware, trash, extra office supplies and coins. Keep items to a minimum, storing only the ones used regularly.

More Crafty Storage Solutions

Creating storage for craft and hobby items can be quite challenging. What to do with all those parts and pieces? Here are some of my favorite tips...

Use a bedroom closet to create a niche for crafting or sewing. The doors can be closed to hide your work in progress. A folding screen can also easily disguise a work area.

A card table or metal banquet table stores under the bed when not in use. This is great if your hobby room doubles as a bedroom. Or use a large piece of plywood over the spare bedroom mattress as a workspace. This can be stored under the bed when guests visit.

The main purpose of eliminating a junk drawer in your home is that it's like a miscellaneous folder in your file cabinet; it gets too full too fast, and it's one of the last places you would look for something. That's why organizing professionals and efficiency experts have been so prejudiced against junk drawers in the past. But if you use it sparingly, promise to clean it out once a month, and stop pouring when it's full, it's okay to keep it.

Pretty Functional
Since counter space is at a premium, don't display all your kitchen knickknacks on the countertop. Hang pictures rather than resting them on easels. Store tall utensils such as wooden spoons, spatulas, whisks and pancake turners in pottery crocks or your favorite pitcher. This makes your favorite things do double duty, creating more drawer space and reducing countertop clutter. Use plastic or wicker in-baskets to utilize more counter space. Don't spread; stack. Purchase wire shelves for pantries and cabinets at your discount store. These shelves literally double cabinet space for dishes, pots and pans. Lid organizers and baking tray racks conveniently store stackable pots and pans in a corner or can be attached to the inside of your cabinet door.

By using some of these kitchen-organizing tips, you will reclaim storage space and cut down on the clutter in your kitchen. Keep your eyes open for storage containers and get creative with flea market items. Remember that one man's trash is another's clutter buster.

HOME MANAGEMENT 101

THE ORGANIZED COLLECTOR

I believe there is a packrat hidden deep inside many of us. Whether you call yourself a packrat, collector or someone who is always prepared for someday, you need a way to effectively organize your treasures.

Interior design teaches a good rule for displaying collectibles: consolidate for a dramatic statement. Gather up all your scattered birdhouses, duck decoys, antique fishing lures, silver platters, photos, figurines or whatever, and then creatively group them together in one place. I think you will be pleasantly surprised at the achieved effect.

Follow the lead of our Victorian ancestors and reduce the need for frequent dusting by displaying your collection under glass. They were truly the great collectors. Use shadow boxes to hang small items together, or to group photos on the wall. Streamline the effect with matching picture mats and frames, eliminating visual clutter and providing the eye with continuity.

Be sure to keep an inventory of your collection for insurance purposes, whether it's children's videos or your prized jazz CDs. Prepare a detailed list of the items, date purchased and amount paid. Create a simple form for your inventory on paper, computer software or use your camcorder to record a video of your collection. Store your inventory in a safety deposit box or at work so that it can be easily accessed in case of theft or natural disaster.

Chapter Four

The Organized Parent

What is the secret of an organized parent? Is it sending your kids to school in clothes with sharp creases, never packing junk food in their lunchbox, and living the perfect life each and every day? I don't think so, but if you ever meet the person I described, please introduce us! Being organized is far from being perfect, and I strongly prefer organization to perfection any day. Organization prepares us for life's twists and turns, and helps us go around them to take an alternate route. Perfection, on the other hand, simply does not allow room for deviation, and since life is full of obstacles and hazards, I simply cannot imagine trying to live that way.

Quite simply, being an organized parent means that you are trained, tooled and transported into the busy world of Parenthood. That includes spilled milk in nice restaurants, moldy French fries under the seat of your new minivan and finding spit-up down the back of your shirt *after* you arrive at your destination. Far from the perfect world you dreamed of while playing house and dolls many

HOME MANAGEMENT 101

years ago, isn't it? Training yourself in the skills of home organization will arm you with the tools you need to fight the enemy head on. Always be prepared for the worst, or what can go wrong will go wrong. So carry extra ammunition with you, so that you're prepared for anything in the battle ahead.

> **Bright Idea # 26**
>
> Keep a stash of non-perishable snacks and drink boxes in the car to save emergency stops at drive-through restaurants.

Use your creativity and follow your gut instincts, because when it comes to the job of raising your kids, you *are* the expert.

POWER WHEELS: 10 STEPS TO ORGANIZING YOUR MOBILE LIFE

Organizing your car is not just for the ultramodern high-tech gadget guru anymore. Move over, high-tech junkies—the organizationally challenged are rising up, and they're on a budget.

Some of my clients literally live from their cars. That is not to say that they camp out with sleeping bag, pillow and lantern, but rather *live from* their cars. Many of us spend more time in our cars than at corporate headquarters or in our home office, creating the need for product storage, a compact filing system and organized desk space.

Car organizing is not limited to those working outside the home either; many a soccer mom dreams of a leisurely commute without library books and sports gear rolling around in the back of the minivan.

The tips that follow can help you create a mini-filing system, store product literature and product samples, stash groceries and organize all those items needing to be mended or returned during your daily outings.

STEP ONE: What's Your Hang Up?
File important papers in hanging files in a portable crate. Prevent the crate from sliding during travel by placing a fluffy towel beneath, or place it in the floorboard where it cannot tip. It's a great way to organize permission slips, contracts, church bulletins, kids phone numbers, sale flyers, coupons, memos and more. (Be sure to keep business and personal records separate so there are no surprises in the boardroom.)

STEP TWO: Read Between the Lines
Carry a To-Be-Read folder with you for review during traffic jams or while waiting for an appointment. This is one of my favorite time-savers that reduces stress at the same time.

STEP THREE: It's All in the System
Create a follow-up system using a notebook with pocketed dividers, a simple recipe box or accordion file. Number the dividers 1-30, and file documents (or note cards) behind the appropriate date of the month for future action.

STEP FOUR: What's on the Agenda?
Consolidate important notes into a daily planner, spiral notebook, calendar or small wipe-off board. If you post a master-planning calendar at home or in your office, carry a spare in your car for

HOME MANAGEMENT 101

taking notes. Remember to consolidate these each day to eliminate overlooked appointments and special days.

STEP FIVE: Mobile Desk
For bills and other correspondence, buy a notebook and fill it with twelve pocketed dividers, one for each month of the year. Label each with birthdays, anniversaries and billing due dates, then fill with correspondence. The binder can be used as a portable desk, or can be stored at your work area. Don't forget to stick your favorite writing pen in the front pocket.

STEP SIX: Improved Storage Space
Keep a large sturdy crate or laundry basket in your car to contain product samples, grocery bags, dry cleaning, library books or rented videos. Invest in two so that you can carry a full one into the house, saving wasted trips from car to kitchen or office. My all-time favorite is a collapsible plastic crate that takes up very little space when not in use.

STEP SEVEN: Detailing
There are a number of visor and glove compartment

Bright Idea #27

Keep an activity box in the backseat for your child. Stock it with pens, paper, crayons, books and a clipboard. While you're at it—keep an activity box for yourself! Put some stationery and nice pens for writing letters, reading to catch up on, and anything else that suits your fancy.

THE ORGANIZED PARENT

organizers available to hold pens, paper, sunglasses and loose change. Make a habit of putting your small items here after each use so you can find them easily.

STEP EIGHT: Expanded Leg Room
Increase limited floor space by hanging pocketed organizers on the back of your front seat to hold maps, brochures, product literature, umbrellas, business cards, tape players and snacks for those long days away from home.

STEP NINE: Our Compact Model
Create a compact office-on-the-go by filling a zippered pencil case with office supplies for your briefcase, tote bag or car. Store basic desk drawer items such as: letterhead and envelopes, business cards, brochures, postage stamps, calculator, pads of paper, pens, pencils, stapler and staple remover, scissors, tape dispenser, rubber bands, paper clips and change for parking or tolls.

> **Bright Idea #28**
>
> Keep the following checklist in the outer pocket of your diaper bag. Use it to quickly assess supplies on hand and supplies needed. With everything on your mind—don't leave anything to chance!
>
> Diaper Bag Checklist
>
> ☐ Medicine
> ☐ Extra powdered formula and water
> ☐ Pacifier
> ☐ Change of clothes
> ☐ Diapers
> ☐ Wipes
> ☐ Changing Pad
> ☐ Burp Pad
> ☐ Receiving Blanket
> ☐ Small toy
> ☐ Breast Pads (if nursing)
> ☐ Clean Shirt for Mom or Dad
> ☐ Gallon-sized plastic bags

HOME MANAGEMENT 101

STEP TEN: Emergency Road Care
Assemble first-aid supplies, a fire extinguisher, large towel or blanket, jumper cables, basic toolkit, rain poncho and a change of clothes. If this sounds like someone's mother telling you to always be prepared, you're right! Experienced parents realize the value of a change of clothes for their kids, but seasoned travelers know how miserable it can be delivering a speech while in wet clothes from a downpour.

Using everyday items to organize our briefcases, cars and offices on the go will not only improve our effectiveness on the job, but will reduce much of the stress we encounter along the way. Happy trails!

ORGANIZATION FOR THE NEW PARENT

Having a baby is a wonderful time in a parent's life, but it is also very stressful. Even the most organized individuals turn into quivering jelly when faced with the responsibilities of a new baby.

If you plan ahead, are prepared for almost anything, and keep your baby care package up to date, you should be a few steps ahead of the game.

Organizing the Diaper Bag
Make a checklist to keep in your diaper bag. Gather these items together, grouping them by related category: food, extra clothes,

toys, diapering and medicine. As a new parent, it's better to have too much than too little until you get the hang of things.

Upon your return from an outing, pull your checklist from your bag and restock your supply. Put the diaper bag in the same location each and every time you finish with it.

Notes from a First-Time Mother
Carry a backup supply of powdered formula (pre-measured) to use in case of emergency. When my son was going through growing spells, I would often miscalculate the amount of bottles to take with us. He would cry for milk until I stopped at the store for more, or cut my visit short to come home. My newly organized husband suggested carrying a supply in a zippered bag—just in case.

Organizing On the Go
Use your car as a traveling nursery. Keep a stroller in the trunk of your car rather than dragging it back and forth from the house. There's nothing worse than getting to the mall or park and finding yourself without a stroller when you need one.

Pack a duplicate of your diaper bag to stash in the car. If you received several diaper bags as gifts, just stash them away for awhile. As your baby grows and his needs change, you may find yourself using a different bag for different circumstances: larger bags for a long day at the babysitter's, and smaller totes for short trips.

HOME MANAGEMENT 101

HOLIDAY OR-
GANIZING TIPS

While shopping for treats for my son's spring party, I spied a display for motivational books and thought: *Wow, that would be a perfect Christmas gift for Grammy, and Aunt Sherry would love the audio tape version.* Before I knew it my shopping cart was full and my shopping was almost completed before it began. Not too bad for mid-April!

What does this have to do with getting organized, you ask? It's simply another effective way to implement my favorite time-management tool: multi-tasking or doing more than one thing at a time.

Our mothers and grandmothers knew about year-round shopping and gift giving. Many of their gifts were handcrafted and they couldn't very well decide to knit an afghan or sew a quilt the week before someone's birthday. They had to make a plan in advance and follow a schedule. For those lucky enough to give store-bought gifts, frugality often played a major role. The budget could

---

Bright Idea #29

Create a list of people for which you need to buy gifts, type of occasion, amount to spend, date of the occasion and gift suggestions. If you need particular hints such as favorite books, music, wine selections or shirt size, then make a note of these too. Store the list on your computer to streamline the process, creating it once, rather than over and over again each year. Keep a copy in your planner or wallet for quick reference. (Tip: listen for hints and write them down throughout the year to ensure you're buying that perfect gift.)

be managed by planning for gifts year round, setting aside a few dollars each month for gifts for friends and loved ones.

Maybe you don't need to be as frugal with your family's money as much as you need to budget the time spent shopping. I think you will find one or two of the following tips useful in your own gift-giving system:

'Tis the Season

Keep ahead of the season by looking beyond your calendar and following the lead of your local retailer. Today you may be wearing long-sleeved shirts and a jacket, but summer clothes are already on display in the malls and mail-order catalogs. Take advantage of the newly stocked shelves, shop pre-season sales and stay ahead of the crowd by thinking like a merchandiser.

It's the Thought that Counts

Making homemade gifts is no longer limited to college

Bright Ideas #30 & #31

Tips for Stress-Free Holidays

1) Stock your freezer and pantry during the month so you will have fewer trips to the grocery and fewer meals to prepare. In fact, this might be a good time to cash in those pizza coupons.

2) Screen your phone calls, then plan a time when you can return them. Wrapping gifts or stuffing cards into envelopes is a good multi-tasking chore to do while you're on the telephone or watching television.

students or cub scouts. For those people "who have everything," give a handcrafted gift this year. I promise you that it will truly be one-of-a-kind. These days, the people on your gift list seem to be increasingly more difficult to buy for; when they need something, they tend to buy it for themselves. Consider giving them something they really need but won't give themselves, like time. Offer to baby-sit their kids, wash or detail their car, deliver a home-cooked meal; use your imagination to give a gift beyond the silk tie or silver-shoe-horn this year.

Many of these tips apply not only to winter holidays but also year round: birthdays, anniversaries, weddings, Valentine's Day and religious holidays. Think outside of the gift box this year, and produce a unique gift from the heart that shows that you put effort into it. Your heart and wallet both will benefit from the fullness of your thoughtfulness, and you won't find your gift lost amid the shuffle.

Stress management and family counselors advise us that the holidays are a season, not merely a day or two. So slow down, time your visits, and spread them out over a few days. Avoid conflicts of where to spend the holiday this year by sharing the season with your extended family. Perhaps you can celebrate Christmas as a family reunion, as many large families do. Pool your resources to rent a hall so that no one has fifty grandchildren running through a formal living room. Donate your old decorations, serve dinner potluck style, and avoid the burden of entertaining-the-masses being heaped on a single person this year.

Money Management

Another way to avoid the holiday blues is to set a gift budget. I won't teach you an in-depth course in Finance 101, but setting a per-gift limit, shopping year round, and making your own gifts are techniques that keep us from feeling so depressed when that credit card bill arrives in January. Here are a few tips to give you a jumpstart on the holidays.

> **Bright Idea #32**
>
> Plan your parties and holiday meals well in advance. Being a parent means multi-tasking, and you're getting better at it every day, but you are only human. If it's not on the list, it probably won't happen.

Greeting Cards: A big time saver is to order holiday cards the first week of October from a mail order catalog, then address them the week of Halloween. By November, you're ready for gift buying and have a major chore crossed off your to-do-list.

Buy holiday cards after the holidays when they are on sale, stashing them away until next year. I suggest you don't pack them away with other holiday decorations because you may forget about them, and you also won't have easy access for advance processing.

Create a permanent record of holiday cards that you have sent and received to avoid making a new one each year. (This is especially important if you buy cards in advance.) Make a list and file it in your file cabinet, on your computer or in a dedicated Christmas Card Record booklet. (These can be found at stationery stores and bookstores or from mail order catalogs.) This allows

HOME MANAGEMENT 101

you to take an inventory of cards for the next year, according to your revised list.

Send postcards instead of holiday cards to save time and postage. Mail cards only to out-of-town friends and family. Send virtual cards electronically. (Of course, this only works for those friends and family members with access to the Internet, but it saves a lot of money and you can send more cards than you normally would.) Order postage stamps through the mail to avoid standing in a long line at the post office.

Have an Open House: Invite friends and family to drop in during a limited time period. An Open House prevents you from spending the holidays traveling place to place, and adds to the time available for loved ones.

Bright Ideas #33 & #34

Have a Tree-Trimming Party: invite friends or family members over, play holiday music to set the mood, serve refreshments or order pizza. It's much less of a chore when everyone pitches in to help. After the holidays, you can do the same thing. No one really likes to un-decorate, but if you make a party of it, to celebrate the New Year perhaps, time passes much more quickly.

Lower your expectations: don't feel you have to be ready for *House and Garden* magazine to photograph your holiday dinner. Potlucks and no-frill meals are wonderful, as most veteran parents will agree. New moms and dads are so overwhelmed with schedules and their beginner role as parents that the last thing anyone expects is a perfect presentation.

Use Your Best Talents: Don't try to do it all when you entertain. If you are a fantastic hostess, then spend your time mingling and making your guests comfortable instead of cooking. Order cold food trays from the deli or hot meals from your favorite restaurant. If you love to cook but hate decorating, ask a friend to help you in exchange for some fresh-baked goods. Florists and interior designers will decorate your home for the holidays, or you can hire a college student from the art or drama department for a small fee. (They also un-decorate, too.)

Call for Help: Hire a mother's helper or sitter to watch the kids as you decorate the house, make appetizers or wrap gifts. Barter with a neighbor to watch each other's kids when shopping for gifts. Borrow, rather than buy, serving pieces from friends or family to keep your December budget under control.

Multi-Task: There's that word again. Most moms and dads do it naturally and business managers practice it without even thinking. Address holiday cards while watching a movie, have the kids put postage stamps and return address labels on the envelopes. Form an assembly line if you can gather enough help. Polish the silver and iron the linen napkins while the pies are baking the day before the big meal, or ask the kids to take inventory of the paper goods for a simple holiday meal.

Plan for Success: It's never too late to make a to-do-list. If you have a planner or calendar, start making notes now. Or grab a spiral notebook and make a list on each page: cards to send, a guest list for an Open House, errands to run, gifts to buy, etc. Plan for the holidays as you would plan for any other event and create a countdown sheet for each day. Remember those wonderful arti-

HOME MANAGEMENT 101

cles in bride's magazines: *How to Organize your Wedding*, and *Count-Down to the Joyous Day?* Use the same strategy by making a to-do-list for each day of the month of December. It's much more exciting to see a list of five things to do each day rather than a long list of 100 things to do this month. Don't forget to cross items off as they are completed; everyone needs a frequent pat on the back.

Avoid the Crowds: Shop during slow periods at the mall such as weekdays or during lunchtime. Avoid the weekend and after-work rush hours. Consolidate your shopping to conserve time and gas. Shop in malls so you won't have to drive far to get what you need. If you've planned and made your lists, you know where to go and when to go there. Start now, shop year-round, or shop at home by direct mail. Today, online shopping is secure, but if you are hesitant to purchase online you can make your selection and then order by phone. Some mail order vendors will wrap your gift and ship directly to the gift recipient. Now that's a time *and* money saver!

Treat Yourself: Don't be afraid to treat yourself and your family to pizza night or what's-in-the-freezer dinners. The last thing you need to do during holiday planning is shop all afternoon or weekend, only to go home and cook a meal. Remember to give of yourself and not just your pocketbook, and stop to smell the gingerbread. As the song says, it's the most wonderful time of the year, so make it a festival from start to finish.

TIME BANDITS

Although there are still 24 hours in each day, you'd never know it by observing today's average home or office. We live in an industrialized nation, one of the most prosperous countries in the world, and yet we are continually robbed of the most precious commodity of all: *time*.

The decade of the 1980s produced efficiency experts, showing us how to keep a time log to chart our work production. Some of you were fortunate enough to attend seminars or retreats to learn how to manage time more effectively. The '80s evolved into the '90s, where power suits were traded in for power tools—we began to dress casually and carry laptops in place of attaches.

> Bright Ideas #35 & #36
>
> *Wooden Cigar Box.* Remote controls multiply; it's a known fact. Even if you use a universal remote for your audio/video system, you still have all those others that need to be used occasionally. Consolidate them into a wooden cigar box purchased inexpensively from a tobacco shop. This solves the question of "where did I leave the remote" and keeps the neat freak in your home happy at the same time.
>
> *Tween Rack.* I wish I had invented this, but the Shakers beat me to it. A "tween rack" is simply an expanding hat rack or pegged rack to hang not-so-dirty clothes. Teens know all about this category of laundry, but it takes parents a little while to catch on to the system.

HOME MANAGEMENT 101

Today, a large percentage of homes, offices and schools have computers available for personal use. Students use beepers and moms carry cell phones. These timesaving tools were brought home from the office to better manage our lives. But who is managing whom here? Are these time savers turning into time bandits?

What would really happen if we didn't answer the telephone during dinner? Would we miss an all-important business call, or just delay a discussion with another telemarketer? Would the world end if you turned off your beeper during lunch in order to focus on the client sitting in front of you (a gentle reminder of Customer Service 101)? Somewhere along the way we have forgotten the purpose of the cell phone, the beeper and call-waiting. They're intended to induce stress or more work? Quite the contrary; they were invented to make routine tasks easier and to simplify our lives. But we must control them or they can easily control us!

These products are not the enemy, but as with other wonderful things in our modern lives, they should be used in moderation. As an organizational consultant, I find myself sympathizing with the working mother who requests a consultation but won't stop talking on her cell phone for thirty minutes to tell me how disorganized her life is. Or the single father who doesn't have any personal time, yet drops his jaw when I suggest he establish house rules for phone calls so the kids are available for cooking and dishwashing chores. It seems so obvious when you're on the outside looking in, doesn't it? But this is your life, too, every frenzied moment of it. And here I am telling you to limit the use of your favorite high-tech toys!

Don't completely do away with these tools, just tweak the user rules a bit. Use the answering machine to screen calls during dinner, meetings, writing sessions, or family conferences—then return your phone calls later. Utilize Caller ID to screen your calls so you don't waste valuable time talking with telemarketers. Use voicemail to discourage solicitors, filter incoming calls and avoid phone tag with business and personal contacts. Implement time savers such as these to pro-actively manage your time--don't just react to others managing it for you.

Time management experts tell us that man cannot truly manage time; it manages us. I'd like to think that we could take a stand against the time bandits, rise above the bells and whistles of laptops, and stop the ringing in our ears. It's time for a change—are you up to the challenge?

Just Say No!

Recently I was gently reminded of the importance of planning and prioritizing projects. I say gently because the reminder was not directed at me but toward my friends and colleagues. I watched a neighbor run back and forth between home and errand-land three times in less than two hours. I saw a colleague add another work project to her already full plate. And I found myself thinking *No wonder busy men and women today are so stressed—we're afraid to say NO.*

What would happen if we said NO and really meant it? Would the sky fall if you didn't bake cookies again for your son's class party? Would the Internet shut down if you were unable to add fresh content to your web site as scheduled? Would your manager

HOME MANAGEMENT 101

fire you for passing on a new project? Most of the time, the answer to these questions is, ironically, NO.

It's very easy for me to pass judgment on these overworked overstressed people, isn't it? After all, I'm an expert in efficiency and time management, conquering clutter and changing people's lives. But the part of me who is a worker, mother, wife, woman, neighbor, daughter and friend shares the same struggle as you each and every day.

Many of us learn better with the help of visual aids, so close your eyes and picture this: a slim attractive mother of three gulping down a Quarter Pounder with Cheese™ in one huge bite, then slurping down a Big Gulp™ in four swallows. Not a pretty picture is it? Wouldn't you like to tell that woman: Slow down, you're going to choke! That burger isn't going anywhere, so eat it slowly and enjoy it!

Now picture that same woman slowly eating her cheeseburger one small bite at a time, savoring each morsel and enjoying the flavor of the grilled hamburger and cheddar cheese. She pauses to take

---

Bright Ideas #37 & #38

ELECTRIC SECRETARIES: Let voicemail or your answering machine be your secretary to screen phone calls, provide outgoing announcements, or put your mind at ease. Turn off the ringer to your cell phone during movies, dinner and time with family.

ERRANDS: Run errands on one day of the week, rather than going back and forth each day. You'll conserve gas and find some hidden time for yourself.

a sip of her soda, taking the time to delicately wipe her mouth with a napkin. She chews her food and enjoys it, one bite at a time.

Get the picture? No matter what the big task is, you can tackle it one bite at a time. Do you need to clean out the garage, but you're waiting for a weekend of uninterrupted time? It's probably never going to happen! But you can clean it an hour each night after you get home from work, and pretty soon it will actually be organized. It isn't going to dissolve into the mist like Brigadoon, so taking your time can't really hurt, can it?

Most organizing projects can be approached using the one-bite-at-a-time method. This is not a revelation or earth-shattering news, but it's refreshing to be reminded of common sense tips now and again. Delegating, limiting interruptions and effective planning are corporate management tools that have been around for ages. Use them in all aspects of your busy lives. Start saying *No Thank You* to those additional tasks handed to you during the course of the day—your plate is already full, now tackle it one bite at a time.

Chapter Five

Office Management 101

"**I**f I had the time to be organized, I certainly would be! There just aren't enough hours in the day for me to get it all done."

Does this sound familiar? It does if you are a busy parent trying to maintain your sanity while balancing work and family. There is so much to do you can't possibly get it all done. Or can you?

As a professional organizer, one of the things that I'm frequently called upon for is to teach others how to organize their time and space. I am here to support, encourage and retrain. You, too, can learn to manage your time and take control of your life with one simple rule of time management: DELEGATE.

Take Turns

Are you the person who always gets asked to bake cookies for your son's teacher appreciation luncheon? Does your neighbor borrow tools from you instead of other handymen on the block? Most of the time, you really don't mind doing things for others and it gives you pleasure to donate your time and talents. But if you find yourself overworked while others are available to lend a hand, or you resent having less time for yourself and your family, then maybe it's time to let others have their turn at contributing and volunteering. Don't be afraid to say no.

Often we say yes because we are afraid of hurting someone's feelings or failing to appear a team player. But in reality, there are usually several others in our group who are willing and able to pitch in when asked. Saying "no thank you, maybe another time" provides others with the opportunity to add their creative flair, feel needed and lighten your workload. Don't worry, there will always be another time–you won't be overlooked just because you once turned down a volunteer position.

Clean as You Go

I've said it before, but I'll say it again…try to clean as you go. On my first day in a marketing job, I visited the kitchen during a coffee break, and read a sign that hung over the sink: *CLEAN AS YOU GO. Your Mother Does Not Work Here!* Cleaning up our own messes forces us to take responsibility for our actions–it's one of the golden rules of kindergarten, right up there with "Don't bite" and "Don't eat paste." So why not pull out that simple rule and re-apply it in your own home and office.

Which chore sounds easier to you: clearing desk clutter or cleaning the office? Would you rather spend your Saturday filing

HOME MANAGEMENT 101

a month's worth of paperwork or resting in the hammock reading the newspaper?

One of my clients had not archived his files for over a year, which for many of you would not be that big of an organizing ordeal. But Victor had three home businesses! His hanging files were overflowing, labeled with vague category names like: insurance, leads and miscellaneous. Not only were they hard to move around in their stuffed file cabinet, he was unable to put his finger on important papers while talking with customers on the phone. For Victor, this was crucial, since he was the sole employee in his businesses, which were all sales oriented. The first thing we did was create an Archive File, here we pulled all non-current files from the previous year, labeled them in manila folders and stored them in cardboard boxes in his office closet. Now he had more file space for past clients that needed follow-up, paid invoices and bank statements. We simply divided those chubby folders into separate categories for each business: INSURANCE became the name of his hanging folder, with Insurance: A Company, Insurance: B Company, and Insurance: C Company as the headings for

---

Bright Idea #39

PRIORITIZE: Use simple tools such as lists to plan your day, and really *use* them to prioritize your time. Don't just make a running list of things to do today, but group them by A, B and C priority. A priorities are things that must be done, B priorities should be done, and C priorities are things that you would (or wouldn't) like to do if you have time during your day.

OFFICE MANAGEMENT 101

his manila folders. He could also have divided his papers by category in the file cabinet with separate tabs and colored folders by company name. He chose the former because his papers overlapped, such as telephone bills, office supplies and so forth. (Check with your accountant or tax advisor for advice on how to maintain your own home office records). Thereafter, he filed on a weekly basis as part of winding down on Friday afternoons when business was slow. He could return a few phone calls before taking a weekend break and manage the paper clutter on his desk at the same time. Straightening a room or workspace before the piles grow too tall keeps work to a bare minimum and reduces the total time you spend on it in the long run.

Try to make a habit of leaving a clean home office or workspace at the end of each day. Close files to prevent lost papers and make your to-do-list for tomorrow. If you work at home, turn down your phone and fax machine to minimize interruptions during time with family. Then close the door and leave your work behind. Creating a to-do list not only prepares you for tomorrow's work but clears your mind and helps you make the transition between work and family.

Bright Idea #40

TO-DO: One of my clients likes to throw in a no-brainer to get herself motivated, such as MAKE A LIST, TURN ON COMPUTER or PULL CHARTS. It's amazing how good you feel about yourself when you see a task crossed off your list!

HOME MANAGEMENT 101

A Space of Your Own

Recent statistics reveal that the average executive wastes 150 hours per year searching for lost documents. One in 20 documents is lost and never recovered. That's a lot of wasted time, isn't it? I can think of a million things I'd rather be doing with my family instead of looking for a paid invoice or the warranty for my broken fax machine. As you re-organize your office or work area there are three organizing essentials to consider:

1. Start with a good plan.
2. Define your space.
3. Utilize whatever storage solutions are necessary to help you keep your papers and products together.

Make plans to set up your office for success. Ask yourself questions like those that follow to help you create a plan for setting up an office conducive to effective work. While expensive furniture and fancy computer hardware is easy on the eyes, it's not always easy on the budget. Plan for what you have now and allow for future growth, and make sure that your plan

---

Bright Idea #41

Making time for yourself allows you to grow as a wife or husband, mom or dad. But it also allows you to grow as a manager or entrepreneur, as you find yourself less stressed and more approachable. If you put self-improvement tasks last on your to-do list, they will remain a low priority. Take time to exercise, develop your career, network with coworkers or colleagues, and enjoy hobbies.

is a practical one.

1. What kind of tasks will you be performing in your office? (writing reports, bookkeeping or teleconferencing)
2. Where will the work actually be done? (at the computer, on a writing desk or sprawled across the floor?)
3. Can you work from home (full-time, telecommuting, occasionally) as easily as in the corporate office?
4. Is there room (literally) in your home for a home office? If not, what can you do to create a corner or niche to work from?
5. What is the budget for your office organizing project? (desk, office supplies, a new chair)
6. What kind of equipment do you currently have available that can be used in your new workspace? (stacking trays, file cabinet, bookshelf, telephone or computer)
7. What is the environment like? (Noise, lighting, temperature)
8. Is there room for growth or expansion? (can you add a dedicated fax line, a second printer or more shelving)

Answering these basic questions will save you a lot of reorganizing in the long run, so make a simple action plan and stick with it.

If you currently have a place to work, read or do paperwork, but it's not the best place to concentrate, then don't keep trying to reorganize it. Too many of us shove an old wooden or metal desk into the office, planning to sit there and work diligently each day. Spare parts have been collected to create an office, and the chair doesn't fit with the desk, so arm strain is an ongoing problem.

HOME MANAGEMENT 101

That's where your plan comes into play. Take a long hard look at what's working (and what isn't) in your own workspace then re-evaluate your system accordingly. Plan an effective space to work for you, your coworkers and assistants (current and future ones). Sometimes the problem is an obvious one overlooked during your haste to carve out a space of your own, but there are always solutions to every problem.

Multi-Tasking

When planning your office space, think about what types of tasks you'll be doing there, whether or not you will be sharing this space with others, and how much area you really need for effective production. Perhaps today you just need a flat surface on which to pay your bills or catch up on business correspondence, but your needs are likely to change in the coming years. Soon you will find yourself needing an overflow area for mailings, a cozy chair for reading trade magazines or a computer and all the peripherals that come with it.

Consider converting a corner of your room into a project area, complete with cafeteria-style table, ample lighting and work stools. Or purchase a sturdy desk with plenty of drawer space for shared office supplies, from scissors

---

Bright Idea #42

LIMIT INTERRUPTIONS: Don't have an open-door policy, screen your phone calls and stick to your rules.

to charcoal pencils. Don't limit your planning process to today's needs, but rather for the next 3-5 years. You certainly don't want to go through this process each time someone assigns you a new project or you receive a promotion.

Apply these same principles of planning and setup to your office at home, too. Whether it's in the kitchen, spare bedroom or a dank corner of the basement, planning ahead will save you remorse in the long run.

Before you rush out to buy new a new desk or computer table, consider the needs of anyone who might use this space. Will a high-back executive office chair work for your short-legged assistant as he sits in front of the computer to update your database? Maybe it's more sensible for you to buy an adjustable mid-back chair instead. Or if he won't use the chair very often, splurge on the chair of your dreams utilizing a back support and foot rest for your junior executive to help him comfortably place his feet on the floor. There's no right answer, just the one you think is going to work for your office several years down the road.

Let's Get Physical

Now that you've jotted down a few ideas about what your office needs are, it's time to take a look at where those needs will be best met. Although you may prefer to set up camp in the main office space near the hub of communication, if this is to be your one and only terminal, reconsider setting up the computer in such busy (and noisy) quarters. Unless you get creative and take over the reception area of your office, there will probably be very little room for a desktop pc, printer, keyboard, mouse, cable and all the good-

HOME MANAGEMENT 101

ies that normally clutter a desktop during computing. However, if you will be using a laptop or PDA (personal digital assistant) to assist you with computations and online work, a smaller corner office will do quite nicely. If your office mate or assistant uses a laptop computer for telecommuting or you need carry work with you on a regular basis, its versatility and compact size will free up your options for corporate office space. A laptop is small, compact and portable. Be sure to create a home for all those accessories that can easily be transported along with the laptop computer to its new destination: a milk crate file box, sturdy tote bag, or a reinforced cardboard box with handles. Just organize your portable office so that you have all your work in one spot, and contain the clutter in one cozy case.

Still not traveling the information highway? Don't need to accommodate a computer for your work area? I have wonderful news! You're not limited in your office planning by telephone jacks, electrical outlets or network connections. Your biggest worry is whether or not you have access to good task lighting and enough wall space for your new desk—you know the one you found in the basement? It's perfect for projects of all kinds, but happens to be seven feet long! Be sure to measure accurately for furniture placement and invest in heavy-duty extension cords for safety's sake.

> **Bright Idea #43**
>
> SHARE THE LOAD: Yes, it's fairly easy to do when you are the boss and it's your job to direct and coordinate people and projects. Take that concept home with you so you can dish out several chores to free up your time.

Form versus Function: Ergonomics 101

Ergonomic specialists recommend a few basic tips before choosing a work surface for computing. First, the keyboard should be in a position where your arms are comfortable and not strained, with forearms horizontal to the floor. Shoulders should be relaxed and not hunched, wrists should be straight. Do not use a wrist rest while entering data, but during rest periods. Place the mouse in close proximity to the keyboard so you don't have to move all over the desktop while working. Adjust the display so that the top of your monitor screen is slightly below eye level for easy viewing. For comfortable reading, your eyes should be roughly 20-24 inches from the computer monitor.

According to Dr. Brad Lustick of Houston, Texas, "The ideal office setup is to start with a good ergonomic chair. Adjust the chair to the person, then adjust the rest of the workspace accordingly. The weight of your legs should rest on the feet, not on the seat of the chair. There should be three inches between the back of the knee and the end of your seat. A tilting seat is crucial to an ergonomic chair because it supports the back during writing or keyboarding and prevents the pelvis from locking and compressing spinal disks.

"Once your chair is properly adjusted, relax your shoulders; bend the arms 90 degrees, and wherever the hands fall is where to place your keyboard. Your computer monitor should be at arm's length, with the top of the screen at eyebrow level. Writing surfaces should be 29-30 inches high.

Invest in a good copy-holder to prevent back strain. Supporting the lower back is like building a strong foundation for the neck.

But leaning forward to read work on your desk does not give good support to your spine.

What if your work environment is not ideal and you have to make do with your desktop or table? You still should purchase a good ergonomic chair and adjust yourself accordingly. Foot platforms support the feet and help in positioning. Adjusting the height of your chair transfers the weight of your body to the feet when you use a footrest. If you work away from your home office for a considerable amount of time, you might consider investing in a support for your back as well.

ORGANIZING YOUR WORK SPACE

After thoughtful planning and then determining where your work area will be, the last step in setting up your office is organizing it. This is always the most fun for my clients, since they can finally look around the house for unused tables, lamps, chairs and make use of all those storage containers stuffed in the attic. Whether you work in a home office or out of the home, getting your office organized is crucial for efficient and effective production.

In the remaining portion of this chapter, I'll provide you with tips for creating an office in your bedroom, kitchen and even your car. From small spaces to large ones, the organizational skills required to make your system keep on working are the same.

Office organization can be challenging for those of us who have limited floor space. Some of us are spreaders, while others are stackers. Whatever your work style, keep clutter to a minimum, label anything you put out of site and consolidate like items as much as possible.

Hot files or work-in-progress can be stored in portable crate systems or in a vertical desktop rack. These are made especially for hanging files, and can easily move from room to room, home to office and back again. Don't overfill, label clearly and have fun finding colorful folders to reflect your personality and style. Neon folders, colored labels or colorful transparent folder tabs separate projects, clients or idea files at a glance. Green could be used for finance, red for red-hot sales leads, blue could be for career ideas or self-improvement, while yellow denotes caution for the credit card bill. Create your own color-coding system that makes sense to you and stick with it.

Hang shoe or jewelry organizers over the doors for office supplies, books and tapes. These can be found constructed of vinyl or canvas and the clear pockets on the front of the vinyl units are invaluable for quickly finding office supplies. If you don't have the wall space or budget for a bookcase, hang

---

Bright Idea #44

Imagine that you must drop a quarter in the coin jar for each time you get up to get a stamp, paper clips or notebook paper. I imagine you're as frugal as I am when it comes to spending your hard-earned cash and wasting your time making unnecessary movements is wasting potential earnings instead. Paying bills promptly saves on monthly penalties, and mailing greeting cards saves on your long-distance phone bills. See the pattern here? Your time really is money in your pocket, so plan to spend it wisely and efficiently.

HOME MANAGEMENT 101

a metal rack over the nearest closet door for holding VHS tapes, cassettes, CDs and computer software boxes. These vinyl-coated organizers found at your home improvement or discount store are inexpensive, lightweight and require no special installation. This portable unit is perfect for small spaces or for those of you living in temporary housing (military or apartments).

Interior decorators encourage us to utilize vertical space. Placing bulletin boards, cork strips or large sticky-notes around the room at eye level provide easy viewing while seated at your desk. Cluster calendars, wall pockets, stationery and shipping products around your work area using the learning center skill you learned earlier in this book.

Keep your office clutter-free by providing a dedicated place for everything. I won't tell you to keep everything in its place, because I don't believe that's humanly possible—not in the home or office. But creating a home for all the bills, paid invoices, cancelled checks and bank statements for your personal or corporate accounts will help you manage the paper clutter faced on a daily basis. Don't just run out and purchase stacking trays for your kitchen counter or desktop without considering their function. Vertical files

> **Bright Idea #45**
>
> Purchase stackable bins for processing paperwork, such as those used for storing vegetables or children's toys. Professional organizer Lisa Kanarek specializes in organizing home offices, and she recommends these stacking bins over the small plastic trays normally used on desks. Not only do they provide you with additional desk space, but they hold larger items such as product samples, binders and crafts.

work much easier for most people than horizontal, especially those who tend to be "stackers" or "pilers". So avoid the horizontal file boxes if you think I'm describing your work habits.

Store hanging folders in file cabinets or use portable crates that store under the desk to keep your desktop as clutter-free as possible. Not only does this provide more room for your papers or computer, it also creates a system that can be moved to another area for filing or reading at another time. It's nice to have a file cabinet or two for storing your files, but certainly not necessary. The plastic crates sold today are made to hold hanging folders, manila folders, binders and just about anything else you can drop into them. If storage space is premium, buy two small crates rather than one large one, so that you can tuck one here and hide one there. One of my clients insists on processing her family's bills at the kitchen table while dinner is cooking in the oven. But before she yells "Dinner!", she hastily shoves her work into a crate, then stores it on top of the clothes dryer behind laundry room doors.

Purchase a drawer divider for stationery and desk supplies to contain the clutter in your drawers. Remember when I gave you permission to keep your junk drawer? I'll let you have a desk drawer, too, if you promise to clean it on a regular basis. Even the smallest of drawer spaces can be expanded into usable space with drawer organizers. Cutlery bins, shallow boxes and items that are bound together with rubber bands or string can be corralled with little fuss or effort. Use whatever you have around the house to calm the chaos, and avoid overfilling the drawer. Clean out your desk drawer at least once a month, taking unnecessary quantities of supplies to the Art Center or (gasp) Junk Drawer in your home. Maybe you're a kleptomaniac and don't realize just how many

HOME MANAGEMENT 101

pens you've collected in that office drawer of yours. Time to confess, Sticky Fingers, and give them up! Let your preschooler practice writing circles and doodles as he tests pens for ink, or teach him how to make a rubber band ball or paperclip chain to amuse him while you're catching up on your filing. Keep on delegating!

Utilize a master calendar or wipe-off board for coordinating special projects. It's not just for the office anymore.

> Bright Idea # 46
>
> Clip or scan articles and then file in a folder for later reading. There's little need to keep the entire magazine, newsletter or report if you can easily clip and file only the information you need. Create a "to be read file" in a pocketed manila folder. Label it, keep it handy and catch up on reading during down times: sitting in the pick-up lane at your son's junior high, waiting on a perpetually late client, or while commuting on the Metro to the office downtown.

Splurge and buy one of those laminated planning calendars. If you spend more time in your home office, or it quickly becomes the family hub where everyone congregates, consider replacing your traditional planner with this new Master Calendar. It doesn't matter how fancy or colorful it is, just buy something that you will keep using and that everyone else can find if they have a question about scheduling. This also saves you a ton of money on office decorating expenses since it takes up so much wall space!

Maintain a workable follow up system with an index card file or accordion file. The dividers are numbered 1-30, and documents (or note cards) are filed on the appropriate day of the month for future action. If you learn only one office management skill from this book, this is the one I hope you truly use. I've used some variation of a "follow up file" since those early days in my first job as a work-study student at college. The system works for multi-tasks, projects or many users. It can be adapted for corporate office, sales projects or home management for tracking rebates. It's portable, inexpensive and it works!

Let's say that you create a portable filing system in the milk crates covered earlier. Using a portable crate with 31 hanging folders (numbered 1-31) or an accordion file with a fold-over flap continues that portable system. After paying bills, mailing cards, buying gifts and making appointments, some of your paperwork will require additional action at a future date. For example, it's hard to make a dental appointment for Timmy on a Saturday afternoon. Place the appointment reminder card received in today's mail in the folder for Monday's date. Monday check that folder to see if there are any items needing your attention. Do this each day of the month at the same time, creating a habit that eventually will become second nature to you. For those items not in the current month, file them either with Day 31 items or in a blank folder at the back of your file. At the end of every month, move the next month's items forward into their appropriate folders. This is probably the most low-tech system I have found that works. Modify it to suit your own needs or find another way to flag important papers needing your attention—just don't let them slip through the cracks.

Go Mobile

For an office on the go, create a portable system for your car or briefcase. Keep a large sturdy crate o r laundry basket in your car to contain product samples. Small hanging file crates securely transport client information or product literature to their destination. Some suggested items for your portable office include: letterhead and envelopes, business cards, brochures, postage stamps, calculator, pads of paper, pens, pencils, stapler and staple remover, scissors, tape dispenser, rubber bands, paper clips and change for parking or tolls. There are a number of visor and glove compartment organizers to contain small items. Pocketed organizers to hang on the back of your car seat are excellent for holding maps, brochures and literature. A compact alternative would be a zippered pouch full of office supplies for your briefcase.

Your Virtual Desktop

Junk email or "spam" can become a thing of the past if you set up your email program to automatically delete incoming junk mails. (Check the user's manual or Help function on your software for this feature.)

Create filters for your computer's in-box to sort messages. You can set up automatic files for: Delete, Read Later and Take Action. If you want to separate email by subject or name, folders can be created for clients and territories. This reduces the time spent each day processing your virtual mail.

Color My World

Color-coding email messages as they arrive in your mailbox helps you prioritize and is a big time-saver. It flags messages from important people and facilitates sorting and organizing. Each software program is a bit different, so you will need to refer to your user's manual or help section of your email software program for complete details. Basically, you just change the settings of your incoming mail by color-coding mail from a particular sender. This saves a great deal of time when wading through email received on a regular basis.

Now that you've set up your personal space, take just a few minutes a day to preserve it Write your to-do list for tomorrow. Straighten your desk before you quit for the day. Purge your files on a consistent basis. Begin each day with a clear desk and a clear mind, and find renewed fervor in the work that brought you here in the first place.

Chapter Six

From Here to There: Effective Time Management

What book on home management would be complete without tips for effective time management? As I mentioned earlier, efficiency experts claim that we cannot really manage time, that it instead manages us. But I do think that with evaluation, planning and maintenance, each of us can solve this mystery once and for all.

What's that you say? You've tried every planning system known to man and womankind and still can't get a grip on remembering birthdays and making it to the dentist on time? You've given up hope and are a lost cause? Nonsense! You've just never found YOUR system. Not my system or your supervisor's or your secretary's, but your very own system for keeping track of all the things going on in your oh-so-busy life. If you learn nothing else from this chapter, know this: everyone has a different level of organizing need. That means that your anal retentive sister may have the need to color-code her sweatshirt collection and alphabetize her spices, but you couldn't care less about those things. All you ask for in life is to pack a lunch for each of your three children and keep track of their extracurricular activities.

Your time management should reflect your level of organizing need, your lifestyle, personality and your life's mission. Without a game plan or mission in your life, you will continue to wander aimlessly through days of missed appointments, forgotten birthdays and unprepared presentations.

Effective time management can be accomplished using three simple steps:

Step 1: Define what's important in your life and that of your family.
Step 2: Schedule time for work, family and self.
Step 3: Design and maintain an effective system for managing time.

Once you have defined your mission and set goals (both personal and professional), scheduling and maintenance will become more visible to you and your daily tasks will take on a whole new meaning.

MISSION ACCOMPLISHED: WHAT'S YOUR PASSION IN LIFE?

Before you balk at the thought of writing a mission statement or going off to a quiet retreat in the wilderness, return for a moment to our four steps of organizing. Remember that the first step in organizing any project is planning, right? And I think you'll agree that LIFE is the biggest project you will undertake. Going through life,

HOME MANAGEMENT 101

day by day, without a plan is like taking off in your car with no map, fuel or compass to guide you.

Realizing you made a wrong turn, landing in the middle of a busy interstate during rush hour, and having no clue where to go next can send the most level-headed driver into a state of frenzy. But if your car is equipped with a compass to guide you, a city and state map to help you find where you are, and a cell phone to connect you with a friendly voice to guide you to your end destination, then the stress level is diminished and your panic lowers to a dull level of discomfort. Relief is almost in sight.

By creating a plan for your life and then arranging the details, you can have a smoother journey. What's your passion? What brings you joy? What is your natural God-given talent that you enjoy sharing with others? It doesn't have to be earth-shattering, such as being a concert pianist or the next Michaelangelo. Perhaps you're a wonderful teacher and have the opportunity to change the lives of hundreds of students. Or you are a whiz at accounting, bringing comfort and relief to the average taxpayer each spring. Perhaps making people laugh gives you a reason to get up each morning. Maybe raising a healthy happy child is all you've ever dreamed of doing and you know without a doubt that will make you completely fulfilled as a parent. Whatever your dream, whatever your gift, define it and make it happen.

I'm a list maker, so writing things down makes them real to me. But if you're one of those people who likes to hear things or say them out loud to make them real, then tell a friend, life coach or counselor. Say it out loud, write it down and make it your own.

In The Happiness Seminar™, professional organizer Sunny Schlenger encourages students to identify what makes them happy in their lives and what's missing in their daily routine. If our lives are out of balance, stress and burnout are the inevitable results. Finding the balance between work and play, routine and spontaneity, being alone and with others, humor and being serious—all these factor into a truly balanced life. Although it sounds too simple to be true, taking the time to do her happiness exercise can change your life and those around you. Write down a list of 100 things that make you happy, whether you currently do them or have done them in the past; watching a sunset, photographing nature, reading romance novels, playing basketball, anything and everything you can think of that makes you happy and brings you pleasure. Keep this list in a place where you can see it and refer to it often.

Take the time to reflect why those things made you happy and how you can bring them back into your life. Too often we forget about ourselves now that we are parents and yet the old adage is true: If Mama (or Dada) ain't happy, ain't nobody happy! Take care of yourself so that you can be the best provider and nurturer your family could hope for.

Goal Planning Made Easy:
Raising the Bar an inch at a time

Now that you've done some soul-searching, and made a wish list of things you like to do, you'll find yourself yearning to do some of those again—perhaps alone, perhaps with your spouse or kids.

Goal planning can be as complicated as attending a business seminar and analyzing your budget, work style and long term planning. Or it can be as simple as writing a few words down on

HOME MANAGEMENT 101

an index card. Use whatever method makes you comfortable to write down a few goals that can easily be attained in a short time. Here are a few ideas to get you started.

A colleague of mine suggested that I create a YES list based on the book *Take Time for Your Life* by Cheryl Richardson. This list has changed my business and personal priorities. I made a list of five things to accomplish in my business and wrote them down on a 5x7 inch card. They are in plain view tacked to the bulletin board over my computer. I read them each day, referring to them as I make my list of "to do's", rewrite my business plan, create a marketing campaign or talk with a client. Each decision I make is based on that YES list, and it's a constant reminder of what truly makes me happy in my career. Writing, teaching organizational skills and other things that are my passion are items on the list. Webdesign, accounting and other detail-oriented tasks that frustrate me are NOT on my list. So if a client asks me to design a website for them, I can quickly glance at my list and be reminded that it's not on my YES list, so I refer them to a contractor rather than do it for them. If someone approaches me about a strategic alliance, no matter how interesting, if it isn't on my YES list, I decline and try to connect them with someone who can help them better than I.

Make your own YES list, writing down five things on a card or piece of paper that involve things that you truly have a passion for. Post it where you can see it every day, and refer to it any time you need to make a decision or stay focused on your goals. Not only does your YES list help you focus, but it helps you set your priorities and stay the course. We can't all be speakers, writers, ac-

FROM HERE TO THERE: EFFECTIVE TIME MANAGEMENT

countants or actors. But we can be our own personal best and this tool will help us stay on that personal path.

Another easy way to set goals is by using a timeline, breaking up future goals into manageable segments. Write down the words 5 YEARS, 3 YEARS, 1 YEAR, 6 MONTHS, and 1 MONTH on a piece of paper. Under each caption, write down a few key words to represent tasks that you would like to accomplish by that time in your life. Refer to your list of 100 things that make you happy and take into consideration that your children won't always be babies needing your constant care. You will grow along with your children and so will the relationship with your spouse. Include career goals, self-improvement and personal needs on this list. For example, in five years, your baby will start full-time kindergarten and you'd like to go back to school. But your happiness list and life mission reminds you that you want to be a full-time mother above all things. So instead of taking four classes and going to school full time, you can plan to take a business course. That's a very attainable goal, but how will you ease this expense into your already tight budget? One of your Three Year Goals could be doing desktop publishing or writing term papers at home for extra money. Save your earnings to apply toward tuition. Perhaps in two years you'd like to enroll Junior in a mother's day out program, so in one year you might begin your research to find a program that is just right for your little one.

See the pattern here? You work forward, backward and everything in between to arrange your goals into a workable system. Nothing complicated, just a simple way of putting some ideas into perspective. Not only are your goals simple ones, but they are attainable. You didn't write down BECOME A MILLIONARE, but you

HOME MANAGEMENT 101

did write down TAKE A COLLEGE BUSINESS COURSE. You didn't make plans to give your child the moon, but you are working toward giving him a head start on his social and cognitive skills by attending a preschool program in the near future.

Goal setting is merely planning for your goals so that they can become factual. Taking baby steps toward the future is the best way I know of to make your dreams a reality. Working around your mission and vision of the future enables you to see the big picture, then you can select activities to help you achieve those goals. The basic to do list you create on a daily basis is merely a compilation of those activities, helping you reach your goal one task at a time.

Balancing Act:
Scheduling time for work, self, and family

Although you hear this phrase quite a bit, learning how to juggle work and family is a challenge that we all face as home managers. If it were easy, there wouldn't be books, magazines, newspaper articles and television shows showing us how to make it more manageable. But you have a head start in the area of life balance since you did your homework. Remember when I asked you to write down your

> **Bright Idea # 47**
>
> Use time blocks - After using the time savers I mentioned earlier, you should be able to really focus on getting one or two of those A PRIORITY tasks accomplished. Not all of them, but some. And if your lists look like that of most of my clients, crossing just ONE thing off your list would be quite a feat!

FROM HERE TO THERE: EFFECTIVE TIME MANAGEMENT

mission, set some goals, and create a "yes" list? Those exercises helped you create priorities, enabling you to know what's most important to you and what you feel is best for your family. The rest of the work can be gleaned from those efforts.

For example, it's difficult to make time for yourself when you've forgotten what makes you happy. You're so busy cooking, cleaning, wiping noses and changing diapers (the every day stuff) that you don't see the big picture. You're lost in the details. But if you've taken the time to plan your goals and created a list of things you would like to do during your life to make yourself (and others) happy, then you can easily schedule your day.

Let's say that taking long warm bubble baths is on your Happiness List. You haven't had that luxury since the baby was born ten years ago, have you? But beginning today, right now, you can plan a time in your schedule for a bubble bath, albeit it a shorter version of days gone by. Perhaps you could take a "time out" after dinner while your spouse or older child watches younger kids. Time for yourself doesn't have to be complicated, but take the time to pencil it into your planner. Make a date with yourself, your spouse, each child in your family, and your friends. Spend time reading a best-selling novel while waiting in the pickup line in front of your daughter's school. Work on a needlepoint project as you watch your kids play in the park. Paint your toenails outside while your toddler splashes in the kiddie pool. This is a wonderful way to recapture those happy moments and is a fine example of multitasking, too!

Setting Priorities: how to tackle the to-do's in your life

Now that you've identified your mission, found things you're passionate about and set some short and long term goals, it's time to tackle the daily grind. How on earth do you accomplish all those to do's in your life each and every day? The only way that you can effectively accomplish anything is to establish priorities. This can easily be done using three categories:

A) Must Do Today (or Vital)
B) Should Do Today (or Important)
C) Would Like to do Today (or Optional)

Whatever your code or terminology, keep it simple and easy to remember. Listmakers will probably want to put an A or 1 beside tasks that must be done during the day, while calendar users will color code their tasks to reflect importance. Colored dots, ink or flags will call attention to must do items of the day. Less important tasks that need to be completed can be listed under must do items, or can be coded with a B, #2, or less flashy colored reminder. Optional or would-like-to-do items can be kept in the main list, in a job jar or on a Honey-Do list on the fridge. Once you've created your system, stick to it so that everyone in your family will know the order of importance.

Just how do you break down the chores and errands and housework when it's never-ending and your lists reads like a Tolstoy novel? My clients who are "creative" or have ADD and are easily distracted, have found that it helps to keep lists short and sweet. There's no way you can do 20 things today, so why not stop your list at 10 or two groups of five? A run-on list of 20 items

FROM HERE TO THERE: EFFECTIVE TIME MANAGEMENT

to do today would make even the most organized home manager want to go back to bed! Break your list into small segments, starting with the week's tasks and working backward day by day until you establish what needs to be done TODAY, what can wait until TOMORROW, what must be done by FRIDAY, and what can wait until spring but needs to eventually be done.

Time Management 101: why most systems don't work

You've bought the best system and been trained in its use. The fancy leather binder, with a plethora of forms and tabs, sits neatly on your kitchen countertop unopened and unused. It seemed like such a good idea the day you bought it, and your sister just loves hers, but you're just not a listmaker. Besides, if you carried that planner around, with your luck you'd lose it! Perhaps you've purchased a fancy PDA, an electronic organizer with all the bells and whistles, but just can't find the time to read the owners manual, and it's just a little too fancy for simple use. Whatever the system, whatever your excuse, you've given up and deemed yourself a failure—a time management klutz, a member of the organizationally challenged. You may be wondering, *What's wrong with me? Why can't I make a simple tool like this work?*

Believe me, there is nothing wrong with you! It's the system that's at fault, not you. Most systems for organizing are based on the designer's preferences, not yours. So if you just happen to process your thoughts the same as the designer of that shiny PDA, then good for you! If not, there are many other options out there just waiting to be tried. Notice that I used the word "options"—there is no "one" way to be organized.

HOME MANAGEMENT 101

Many time management systems use left-brained principles, and are created by and for those who think the same way. Everything is neat, orderly, alphabetize and put away until further notice. But what about those who are creative thinkers (artists, writers, actors) and need visual reminders to stimulate their creativity and memories? Having thoughts neatly tucked away in a closed binder will not help them remember to write a query to a magazine editor or pick up milk from the store on the way home from work. Visual learners need everything out in sight, not closed up in a file cabinet or listed on a piece of paper.

Other systems neglect the other sensory perceptions we use at work and play, such as hearing and speaking. If you are the type who must say someone's name in order to remember it next time you meet, or talk out loud in the shower or while driving, then you are probably an auditory learner, and will not benefit from a traditional time management system. But you can supplement or even replace it with a handheld recorder, to remind yourself of things you need to do and when they should be done.

In her book, *The Way They Learn*, Cynthia Tobias Ulrich teaches us that there are three main learning styles for all children: Visual, Auditory and Kinesthetic. By the time you have finished reading her book, you have identified the learning style of yourself, your children, your spouse and almost everyone you know. It helps solve the mystery of a messy room or unfinished chores if you understand how your child classifies and sorts through problems and tasks to do. A visual learner needs reminders out in plain sight to remind him what to do: backpacks need to be in sight so he won't forget to take them to school, permission slips need to be posted on a bulletin board of clipped to a mag-

FROM HERE TO THERE: EFFECTIVE TIME MANAGEMENT

netic clip on the fridge to remind him to have you sign it, and craft supplies need to be out on the desk so he can see what his choices are to capture creative flow. The auditory learner, on the other hand, needs to tell you all the details of his day, what needs to be done and what he's accomplished. These details are not necessarily the results of an over-talkative child but merely your child's way of processing his to-do's and crossing them off his mental list. Saying is remembering, and helps with problem solving as well. The kinesthetic learner is on the go, pacing while on the phone with his friends, hopping up the stairs as he memorizes his times tables or his ABC's. Doing is learning, and actions speak louder than words.

Another reason why traditional time management systems don't work is that they don't allow for differences in energy levels. Are you a morning person, able to accomplish more before your coworkers arrive at work than during the entire afternoon? Do you set your alarm early to get a head start on chores while your household is still peacefully asleep? Or do you prefer to work late into the evening, catching up on paperwork, paying bills or writing that best-selling novel after everyone else is in bed? Consider your internal clock when creating your own time management system to help you conquer the myth of a one-size-fits-all time management system. Remember to allow for energy levels when scheduling your tasks—if you've been up since five in the morning, and tend to do your best work in the early hours after dawn, scheduling a late afternoon meeting might not be the most productive for your coworkers. Leaving household chores for late night cleanup is not an effective way to make use of your best energy levels either, especially if you fall headfirst into a heap of unfolded laundry on the living room floor! Plan for active success; after all, it's YOUR schedule and no one knows your preferences better than you.

When you factor in all the styles of learning, and the differences in our personalities, it's no wonder that we struggle when trying to find a system to make our lives easier. Working with, rather than against, your style ensures that you will keep using the system you have created, streamlining the organizational process into a smooth-running machine.

DESIGNING AN EFFECTIVE SYSTEM

You've learned how to set goals and incorporate them into daily living, you've learned the relationship between financial planning and balancing your checkbook. You've even learned how to prioritize your to-do's, juggling them around to fit neatly into the unplanned surprises that fill your day.

But how on earth do you translate these skills into a workable time management system for your family? When you were on maternity leave with your first child, you retired your leather-bound planner, never to use it again. As your child grew and adopted a social life of her own, you traded in that planner for a calendar with large squares and a four-color pen. This works fine when you're at home looking at the calendar tacked to the fridge, but what about those times at PTA and Room Mother meetings when you need to check your schedule for conflicting events? You can't very well drag the family calendar to school, work and the dentist.

FROM HERE TO THERE: EFFECTIVE TIME MANAGEMENT

The beauty of creating your own system is that there are no hard and fast rules. Take a binder, calendar, card file or any combination thereof and make it your own. Whether you need to write a list, coordinate your PDA with your computer's planning software, or create a planning calendar for the entire family—create a time management system that is easy to update and keep on hand for optimum use. Tucking your family's schedule away in a remote home office location ensures impending doom, while keeping your schedule in full view for use by all members creates an atmosphere of successful time management.

> **Bright Idea # 48**
>
> Combine software, electronics and notebook schedulers to create your own personal planner. Don't be afraid of modifying a professional designed system to make it work especially for you.

Although there are many types of time management systems, they fall into three main categories, with pros and cons for each. Choose from one or any combination of the three listed below:

Manual Planner
Whether you invest in a costly binder or create one of your own from a file box full of index cards, the manual planner is a system of lists and contacts noted on paper, constantly moved forward until complete.

Create a planner from a loose-ring notebook, dividers with tabs and lined notebook paper. Add pocketed dividers and you have a

HOME MANAGEMENT 101

customized planner to hold any size of handout, flyer or permission slip.

Purchase a planner from FranklinQuest™, DayTimer™, BusyWoman's™ Daily Planner or any of the numerous commercial systems created for busy people just like you. Browse through the filler pages, choosing forms and checklists that fit your lifestyle. Sizes and patterns vary, so shop for a planner as you would a briefcase or new purse. What's your lifestyle? If you're mostly using it in an office or at a desk, a large size is good for tabletop viewing and holds many months' worth of tasks at a time. But if you're in the field (sales or marketing), travel a good deal (professional speaker), or don't carry a briefcase (full time mother), consider a compact size instead.

When filling your planner, start with the basics and then expand as time and need permits. Essentials for startup include: a to-do list, monthly calendar, yearly calendar (to see the big picture and plan projects), and a section for current projects. Later you can add contacts (telephone, address, email) and a place to record expenses.

Computer Software
Although we may never truly be a paperless society, we can take a step in the right direction by keeping our contact information and calendar on our computer. From database management to email software, there is something for every level of need you may encounter. If you are already using a contact management system at work, and it's easily adaptable for personal use, don't hesitate to use it at home as well.

FROM HERE TO THERE: EFFECTIVE TIME MANAGEMENT

The advantages are easy to recognize—you already have a system in place, know how to use the program and spend most of your time on a computer. If you routinely back up your data, you don't have to worry about losing important details of your life, and it can easily interface with your husband's PDA and your son's laptop. Some time management systems print out pages to go into a manual planner should you need to carry your contact information with you or switch systems at a later date. Many have alarms, and multi-user capabilities, and move unfinished tasks forward automatically.

Electronic Planner
Small and portable, the electronic planner offers the automation of a computer and the flexibility of a manual planner. Palm Pilot, Handspring, Sharp Wizard and other handheld devices provide almost unlimited use of modern technology to keep you on task. Electronic planners are great for those of you who don't like to write lists, have problems using a right-handed notebook binder or can't read your own handwriting. Expansion slots and cradles allow for easy integration with the computers at work and home, while reminding you to routinely back up your data. Not only do you have all the features of a basic planner, such as calendar and contact information, but many newer models incorporate gaming and email capabilities as well.

If you are not into high-tech, then learning to use all the features of your electronic device may make you shudder. The cost is much higher than a traditional planner and if it's dropped or stolen, you've lost a considerable investment of time and money. Some older or lower-end models are not expandable, have dedicated

HOME MANAGEMENT 101

software and a short battery life. So if you forget to back it up and your batteries die, you're on your own. But if you need a liaison between work and home, something that will consolidate your work schedule with your home life, buying an electronic planner may be just what you need to balance your time.

Routine Matters

Hopefully, your new time management system is in place and you're quite pleased with the fruits of your labor. You've planned, prioritized and organized your life into one neat compact scheduler. But if you don't use it on a regular basis, you might as well store it in the attic or leave it unopened in the box in which it was shipped. Since it takes an average of 21 days to establish a habit, starting a new plan only to give up after a few days is defeating yourself before you even get started. Stick with your new system for three weeks, and if it's simply not working the way you envisioned, then it's time to tweak, tug and remold.

One of my colleagues, Harriet Schechter the Miracle Worker, says that "life is 5% joy, 5% grief, and 90% maintenance." If that doesn't inspire you to keep up your new system, nothing will!

Chapter Seven

It's A Dirty Job, But...

We can run, but we can't hide. No matter how many stars we wish upon, some organizational and dirty jobs don't cease to exist. Spring cleaning and bathroom maintenance are the two chores most commonly loathed. In this chapter, we'll try to take some of the drudgery out of these cleaning culprits.

Using the words bathroom and family in the same sentence seems like an organizing nightmare just waiting to happen. Not only is the bathroom probably the smallest room in your home, but you probably have more than one. So multiply any organizational challenges by 2 or even 3 and... well, I think you get the picture and it isn't pretty!

At the turn of the century, bathrooms inside the home were new to homeowners; builders and designers steered clear from wood trim and casings. The look was clean and spotless, and the move toward a more sanitized germ-free life descended upon us. White tile floors supported white porcelain sinks and tubs, free-

HOME MANAGEMENT 101

> **Bright Idea # 49**
>
> In the garage, hang wood lathe strips high on the inside walls, then attach long nails or clips to store long-handled tools. Use bike hooks hung from the ceiling to store bicycles at the season's end. Mount inexpensive pegboard to the wall, adding hooks and clips for all the tools that seem to mysteriously disappear. Freestanding drawer units purchased at garage sales provide drawer storage for flat items. Recycle the tip you learned from your woodshop teacher, and affix jar lids to the bottom shelf of a cabinet with screws or nails, then add the jar full of nuts, bolts and screws. Recycle margarine tubs and whipped topping containers for holding tapes, coils of wire and screws. Invert an old barstool or dilapidated trashcan to hold tall items such as baseball bats, fishing poles and hockey sticks.

freestanding and simple. But there went the storage spaces gained with built-in cabinetry and easy maintenance. All that white combined with a houseful of muddy husbands and sandy preschoolers does not make for a happy equation.

Many homes today still suffer from storage shortages, especially in the bathroom. If there IS a linen closet, you're often limited to one per bathroom, or it's located down the hallway. But it's really not quite as scary as you think to plan, organize and maintain a small bathroom (or two or three). Shedding hair, foggy mirrors, wet floors and damp towels happen to the best of us, and there are ways to contain the clutter your family creates each and every day.

BATHROOM BASICS

Surviving the morning rush hour in any busy household is no easy feat, especially if you and your family are sharing bathroom space.

Organizing tips for small spaces easily reduces bathroom clutter. Utilizing vertical space, minimizing towel usage and creating a home for dirty laundry greatly reduces the clutter your family creates each time they leave the bathroom.

Toss It or Stow It

To keep clothes from covering your entire bathroom floor, place a large hamper in the bathroom. If you don't have enough floor space for a freestanding unit, buy one to hang over your door or on the doorknob. These mesh or canvas bags are washable and can be taken down on laundry day.

For those not-quite-dirty clothes, encourage family members to carry those back to their bedrooms for hanging. Some people prefer not to hang gently worn clothes on hangers or return them to drawers. An alternative is to use a

> **Bright Idea # 50**
>
> Reduce the number of towels your family uses by encouraging your crew to use a towel more than once. Color-code the towels so that each person knows which one is theirs. At the very least, use one towel during the week to dry wet hair. Two towels per person times seven days a week... well, you do the math. That adds up to a lot of laundry!

HOME MANAGEMENT 101

"tween rack," as mentioned earlier, hung in the closet or on the back of the closet door solely for this purpose.

Pack It In

Try creating vertical storage space in your bathroom. Utilize stacking bins, over-the-toilet shelving, hanging produce baskets, or any type of container you can think of to store the necessary toiletries for yourself and your family. Color-coded systems work extremely well for toothbrushes and hairbrushes. Try to have a family shampoo and toothpaste so that you don't have duplicate items taking up valuable space around the vanity.

If you rent your home or apartment and want to avoid a permanent installation, purchase holders with suction cups for managing tooth-brushes, soap, shampoo and other bathroom items.

In a perfect world, each member of your family would have a bathroom of his own. Foggy mirrors would not be an issue, showers would be of unlimited duration with no thoughts of hot water supply and soggy soap would be a thing of the past. Until that

> **Bright Idea # 51**
>
> Create extra hanging space for wet towels by installing hooks or hat racks on your wall, low enough for even the smallest of family members to use. If wall space is at a premium, purchase an over-the-door towel rack or behind-the-door rack to vertically store towels.

day comes, however, try to incorporate some of the tips just described to simplify your morning rituals, reduce the clutter and lighten your laundry loads.

SPRING CLEANING FOR THE HOUSEWORK IMPAIRED

Each year, on the first day of spring, the pressure to clean and declutter our domicile descends upon us. I will be the first to admit that I get a strong urge for change, but since I'm pretty organized to begin with (it comes with the title), I can let things slide quite a bit. I'll be happy to share a few tips with you if you promise to leave your white gloves at home next time you visit me.

Clean as You Go: I realize this is the mantra of many a professional organizer (as well as most everyone's mother), but it does cut the cleaning time down considerably. If you have a home for papers, toys, clothes, etc. you will have fewer things to pick up and vacuum under when it's time to clean. Cleaning as you go saves time, energy and eye strain.

Dust Bunnies, Beware: Tube socks placed on little hands or a pint-sized feather duster will chase those dust bunnies right off the brick-a-brack and under the rug. There is really no reason to get out the soft cloth diapers and lemon oil if you have a house full of kids and the breakables were boxed up long ago. Even toddlers can help you with this chore if you turn it into a game: Mommy

HOME MANAGEMENT 101

cleans high, Baby cleans low. Before you know it, they're hooked into thinking it's fun and there's no turning back. Use a blow dryer to blast the dust off silk plants and greenery. Toss pillow shams and comforters into the clothes dryer add a dryer sheet, and turn the dial to air. Tackle the toss pillows and afghans next. Things will smell nice and fresh and you'll save a bundle on dry cleaning bills.

Much Ado About Nothing: Perhaps you were once a neat freak, but that was B.K. (before kids). As a parent, you know that having children changes all the rules and your life is never the same. What was once maintained on a regular basis has lapsed considerably in the homes around your neighborhood. Vacuuming, dusting and mopping are actually performed bimonthly or monthly instead of weekly.

In all honesty, when guests visit your home, they are really not there to inspect the dust on your coffee table or to check for vacuum tracks on your pile carpet. Grandma is here to see the kids. Your next-door-neighbor is visiting with her daughter for a play date and she's much too busy redirecting her two-year-old to notice whether or not you mopped your kitchen floor today. So lighten up and don't be so hard on yourself. No one else is!

When All Else Fails, Cheat: Follow the example of professional cleaners and buy products that will do most of the work for you. Cleaning products that are designed to eliminate lime and hard water stains will do just that given half a chance. Don't needlessly scrub without giving the cleaners time to do their job—this can be a great time-saver for you. It also helps you multi-task because

IT'S A DIRTY JOB, BUT...

you can squirt toilet cleaner or mildew cleaner onto the bathroom fixtures and move on to other areas in your house. Return later for a quick wipe and recoup lost time for a story with your kids or to flip through a magazine. Go ahead, don't feel so guilty; you've earned it. Using quick and dirty tricks like these will add a spring in your step and sparkle to your life.

Appendix

More Help for the Organizationally Challenged

Recommended Reading

Clutter's Last Stand: It's Time to DeJunk Your Life! by Don Aslet. Writers Digest Books. ISBN 0898791375.

Conquering Chaos at Work: Strategies for Managing Disorganization and the People Who Cause It by Harriet Schechter. Fireside. ISBN 0684863146.

Conquering Chronic Disorganization by Judith Kolberg. Squall Press, Inc. ISBN 0966797000.

Creative Time Management for the New Millennium by Jan Yager. Hannacroix Creek Books. ISBN 1889262153.

Frozen Assets: How to Cook for a Day and Eat for a Month by Deborah Taylor-Hough. Champion Press Ltd. ISBN 1891400614.

APPENDIX

How to Be Organized in Spite of Yourself: Time and Space Management That Works With Your Personal Style by Sunny Schlenger New American Library. ISBN 0451164695.

How to Raise a Family and a Career Under One Roof: A Parent's Guide to Home Business by Lisa M. Roberts. Unknown. ISBN 0943641179.

Organize Your Books In 6 Easy Steps: A Workbook for the Sole Proprietor Service-Oriented Business by Donna M. Murphy. IRIE Publishing. ISBN 0966484800.

Organizing Your Home Office For Success : Expert Strategies That Can Work for You by Lisa A. Kanarek. Blakely Press. ISBN 0964347016.

Organized to be Your Best! Simplify and Improve How You Work by Susan Silver. Adams Hall Pub. ISBN 0944708617.

Organizing from the Inside Out: The Foolproof System for Organizing You Home, Your Office and Your Life by Julie Morgenstern. Owl Books. ISBN 0805056491.

Home-Based Business Mom : A Basic Guide to Time Management and Organization for the Working Woman by Julie Shulem. Newhoff Pub. ISBN 0966157818.

Practical Home Office Solutions by Marilyn Zelinsky. McGraw-Hill Professional Publishing. ISBN 0070633657.

Taming the Paper Tiger at Home by Barbara Hemphill. Kiplinger Books. ISBN 0938721577.

The Family Manager by Kathy Peel. Word Books. ISBN 0849939372.

The Tao of an Uncluttered Life: Lao Tzu's 10 Principles for Organization by Karen Hicks, Steve Allen. Humanics Pub Group. ISBN 0893342939.

HOME MANAGEMENT 101

The Way They Learn by Cynthia Ulrich Tobias. Focus on the Family Pub. ISBN 1561794147.

Time Management for the Creative Person by Lee T. Silber. Three Rivers Pr. ISBN 0609800906.

Organizing Products

File Solutions Organizing Systems for home, students, and home office. Each kit includes a FileSolutions® guidebook, FileIndex®, and pre-printed labels. FileSolutions, PO Box 516381, Dallas TX 75251-6381, Phone: 972-488-0100 Email: fsservice@filesolutions.com, www.filesolutions.com

EZPocket Organizers™—Keep weekday or project files close at hand for easy review and retrieval. Grommets make it easy to hang these organizers anywhere and free up valuable horizontal space. EZ Pocket, 1191 South Yosemite Way, Suite #47, Denver, CO 80231, Phone: 800-681-8681, Email: ezpocket@ezpocket.com, www.ezpocket.com

Mom Central—Think of Mom Central as everything a Mom knows filed and spiraled between two covers. A beautifully designed book filled with hundreds of lists that will help you organize your busy life with kids. Mom Central, Mail Orders: 440 Beacon St. Chestnut Hill, MA 02467, Online Orders: www.momcentral.com or www.amazon.com

Post-it® Flags—A convenient, effective way to flag and index information, Post-it® Flags come in a variety of attention-grabbing colors, sizes and pre-printed messages. Choose an action-oriented pre-written flag or get creative and write your own. 3M Company, Available at Staples and

APPENDIX

Office Max stores nationwide, Order online at: www.3m.com/Post-it Phone: 888/364-3577

Homework Helpmate—This caddy holds all homework supplies including folders, pencils, glue, scissors, etc. in a portable holder--great to store supplies in and easy for kids to carry to the kitchen table or other "desk" area. So Organized!, Ltd, a professional organizing service, 53 High Hollow Rd., Roslyn Heights, NY 11577, Phone: 516/625-8981, E-mail: SOrganized@aol.com, www.b-organized.com

Special Days—Each undated page provides the month and the days, printed on a convenient pocket for storing your cards. So Organized!, Ltd, a professional organizing service 53 High Hollow Rd., Roslyn Heights, NY   11577, Phone: 516/625-8981 ,E-mail: SOrganized@aol.com, www.b-organized.com

6-Drawer Office Chest: Excellent storage item for the office as well as home. File chests feature removable casters, drawer stops and tabs to attach chests together. Stacks & Stacks, 1045 Hensley St., Richmond, CA 94801, Phone: 877/278-2257, Fax 510/215-5993, www.stacksandstacks.com

Mug Rack: Solid wood mug rack is designed to mount to the wall. Features a shiny protective lacquer. Pegs have a detent on them to stop items from falling off. Available in 4 and 6 peg versions. Hardware not included. Stacks & Stacks, 1045 Hensley St., Richmond, CA 94801, Phone: 877/278-2257, Fax 510/215-5993, www.stacksandstacks.com

HOME MANAGEMENT 101

Collapsible Crate: This crate easily expands from its folded position. Use it in your trunk, closet or office. File rods available for letter size file folders. Stacks & Stacks, 1045 Hensley St., Richmond, CA 94801, Phone: 877/278-2257, Fax 510/215-5993, www.stacksandstacks.com

Online Organizing Solutions

B-Organized: organizing tips and tools, www.b-organized.com

California Closets: closet design and installation for your home, www.calclosets.com

EZ Pocket: hanging pocket organizers for the week, month or current projects, www.ezpocket.com

Get Organized: storage products for home and office, www.getorginc.com

Lillian Vernon: organizing products for parents and teachers, www.lillianvernon.com

OfficeMax: supplies, furniture and storage containers for home and office, www.officemax.com

Organization, Etc: practical and decorative solutions for organizing your home, www.org-etc.com

Rubbermaid: durable storage containers for your home, inside and out, www.rubbermaid.com

Stacks & Stacks: organizing products for home and office, www.stacksandstacks.com

The Container Store: products and designs to organize closets, kitchens and more, www.containerstore.com

APPENDIX

HomeOrganization.com: discount organization and storage products, www.homeorganization.com

What's on the Agenda?

At a Glance: planning products and calendars, www.at-a-glance.com

Day-Timer: time management system tools, www.daytimer.com

FranklinCovey: solutions for boosting personal and business effectiveness, www.franklincovey.com

The Busy Woman's Daily Planner: time management strategies & tools for busy women, www.thebusywoman.com

Your Virtual Desktop

CyberContact: contact and information manager for internet users, www.liraz.com/cybercontact

Eudora Place: management tool for your email, www.eudora.com

Paper Management

FileSolutions: color-coded Organizing Systems for home, students and home office, www.file-solutions.com

Taming the Paper Tiger Software: computer indexing system for paper management, www.thepapertiger.com

Esselte: office filing products including Pendaflex folders & Dymo label makers, www.esselte.com

HOME MANAGEMENT 101

Around the House

Cheapskate Monthly: monthly newsletter for debt-free living, www.cheapskatemonthly.com

Martha Stewart Living: tips and products for home living, www.marthastewart.com

Miserly Moms: frugal tips for living on one income, www.miserlymoms.com

The Clean Team: cleaning experts share their tips, www.thecleanteam.com

The Dollar Stretcher: online magazine for simple living, www.stretcher.com

The Tide Clothesline: laundry and stain removal tips, www.clothesline.com

OrganizedTimes: organizing solutions for your busy life, www.organizedtimes.com

Travel Aides

Drive USA: tips for driving, car care and road travel, www.driveusa.net

Mobile Office Organizers: automotive office products, www.mobilegear.com

Education & Support

ADDitude Online Magazine: online magazine for people with ADD www.additudemag.com

APPENDIX

Messies Anonymous: support for messies online, www.messies.com

OrganizedUniversity: training for all your organizing needs, www.organizedu.com

The Organized Exchange: weekly organizing e-zine, www.organizedtimes.com

Ergonomics

Backbenimble ergonomic and self care products for your home and office, www.backbenimble.com

Closing Thoughts

Now that you have learned what it takes to become a successful home manager, my wish for you is that you have found *Home Management 101* a practical, hands-on tool to help you get and stay organized in your busy life. Whether you are single, married, have a house full of children or one child, using the organizing principles in this book will launch your new career as a home manager. I've tried to provide you with common sense organizing strategies, rather than create fancy systems that might make you feel defeated before you ever begin your quest for a more organized life.

Keep the lines of communication open with your family, establish your boundaries, don't be afraid of change and stick together. These principles aren't limited to parenting and marriage, but apply to all the aspects of a family's life. Respect one another's space and organizational needs, choose your battles carefully and be as consistent as possible to make your system work. I guarantee it will be worth it when you find yourself the parent of an organized child with good study habits and a need for order.

HOME MANAGEMENT 101

Remember that being organized is a journey, not a destination, and you are teaching invaluable skills to the travelers entrusted in your care. It's not too late for you or anyone else living under your roof to learn these organizational skills. By learning and applying simple organizational techniques at home and work, you are becoming a great role model for your kids and their friends. You just never know who's watching (and learning) from a distance, and if you're not careful, your organizational skills and time management training will rub off on those around you—now that's something to look forward to!

I wish you all the best in your quest for a balanced life. May your organizational journey be an easy one, and your load lightened by those you love.

- Debbie Williams

About the Author

Debbie Williams, owner of Let's Get it Together©, is an organizational strategist, syndicated columnist and educator. Debbie has over 15 years of administrative and training experience, holds a bachelors degree in education and works as a freelance writer for various entrepreneurial and parenting publications from her Texas home. She serves as editor and publisher of the organizing e-zine, The Organized Exchange™, and is the host and founder of the annual Online Organizing Expo: Virtually Organized™.

The founder of OrganizedU©, an online training and support facility, Debbie is dedicated to helping others balance their lives with organizational techniques. You may contact her by email at
debbie@organizedtimes.com,
or visit her web site at www.organizedtimes.com .

To locate a professional organizer in your area, refer to her online Member Directory at: www.organizedu.com/directory.htm. Obtain a free referral by email (info@organizedu.com) or by calling toll free: (877) 859-1585

Enjoy all the time and money-saving benefits of the once-a-month-cooking method... while losing weight at the same time!

You asked for it--and you got it. Deborah Taylor-Hough has created 20+ one-week menus that you can mix and match to create an abundant supply of healthy, easy, freezer meals!

ISBN 1-891400-19-3 Price: $19.95

Healthy Foods:
an irrevent guide to understanding nutrition and feeding your family well
by Leanne Ely, C.N.C.

Plagued by picky eaters? Thinkg "Health Foods" equals "Granola Food?" Do you consider ketchup a vegetable in your child's diet? Help is here. With a humorous touch, Leanne will show you how to make nutrition a priority in your family--without battles at the table. Includes many child and parent-friendly recipes.

ISBN 1-891400-20-7 $19.95